E.I.D.

Entrepreneurial Idiot Disease

6 STEPS TO MAKING $$$ ON FACEBOOK RIGHT NOW!

TODD BATES
JOSEPH BRIDGES
JAMES BRIDGES

600 Million+
Waiting to Help You Now

Published by Todd Bates Publishing Inc, Denver, CO.

ISBN# 978-0-557-67133-5

Book graphics created by Ryan Leisure.

Editing of book by Lauren Sobaje

For additional books in the E.I.D series visit:

www.EIDBooks.com

These remarkable stories are from early entrants who followed the advice you are about to discover.

Dustin Burleson
"★★★★★" The Facebook Twins know how to run a business-to-business system. Great information, awesome service, and accountability for business owners like me who have 9 irons in the fire at any given time. Make the investment with these guys and you will reap the rewards over and over. Highly recommend!
August 17 at 7:48pm · Like · Comment

Renaissance Art
"★★★★★" You guys ROCK!!! Thanks for your continuing help in getting my FB fan page up and noticed, your targeted instruction and above all, the homework with a deadline to keep me moving in the right direction. You create momentum and then help to keep it going.
August 17 at 7:26pm · Like · Comment

Ralph Vargas
"★★★★★" The twins have provided outstanding info, work and customer service thru out the year I have been associated with them. From the webinairs, communication in facebook and my fanpage- facebook.com/RalphVargasRealEs tate- all the work has been top notch and well thought out.
August 8 at 2:03pm · Like · Comment

Caseys Pub
"★★★★★" I want to thank you guys for helping me with my fan page and teaching me techniques I never thought were possible. I have doubled my opt in email addresses and I'm starting to get a lot of feed back from customers. Thanks again and I would suggest your services to anyone.
August 2 at 9:27am · Unlike · Comment

Greg Loll
"★★★★★" Wow what a difference a couple of months make. I follow Joey and James system for my fan page and website and I went from #8 to #1. This was my goal when I started working with them thinking that it may take me a year but to my surprise only a couple of months. These guys know what they are doing and are very easy to work with I would recommand them to everybody who wants to build there business.
July 22 at 4:56pm · Like · Comment

Bill Zoellner I thought it was top of mind awareness
July 22 at 4:58pm · Like

Write a comment...

Philip Larmon
"★★★★★" Where do I start... James and Joey have impacted my life dramatically. So far in life I find very few people that can keep up with my thought process and add tremendous value. I know their strategies work because that is how we met. Now some 3 or 4 years later we still talk on a regular basis. The individual attention and business planning is of huge value to me. The sincerity they approach ...
See More
July 21 at 11:52am · Like · Comment

John H. Fisher

"★★★★★" The coaching sessions with Joey Bridges have been fantastic! Great marketing tips each coaching session that goes beyond Facebook. Joey keeps me focused on completing weekly marketing goals--a huge help.

April 1 at 6:14am · Like · Comment

Mike Boom

"★★★★★" These guys know their stuff - they breathed completely new life into our fan page. Joey and Jamie showed their expertise in sending through a series of sharp posts that we could post on the fan page over a period of time. Invaluable service. Mike http://gebomana.com/

March 9 at 12:36pm · Like · Comment

Bart Baker

"★★★★★"

February 25 at 2:01pm · Like · Comment

Bart Baker Fan Page Marketing set up our page and gave us all kinds of good advice. Now we're applying that advice and building our fan base. I don't think we would have done nearly as well without their help.

February 25 at 2:03pm · Like

Write a comment...

Shelly Eshelman

"★★★★★"

February 24 at 7:58am · Like · Comment

Andrea Flint-Gogek

"★★★★★" Just closed my first deal that I got through a posting on my facebook page that Joey and James did for me!!! A random fan passed the information on to a family member who called me and we closed a cash deal in 17 days! Thanks for the excellent service and guide for my fan page!!

February 23 at 9:28am · Like · Comment

Todd Bates
Thanks to my wife Michele for supporting me through this book. You and the kids, Alex and Morgan, had to deal with all that goes into creating this.

Thanks to all of the clients who contributed their feedback, stories, and ideas to how Facebook has changed their business. This book would not have taken place without you.

James Bridges
Thanks to everyone who supported me while writing this book. My wife for her consistent understanding and support in all of the crazy businesses I have done.

Thanks to my parents who have consistently encouraged me to do my best in all of my endeavors. Your encouragement has helped me to keep pushing the envelope.

And thanks to my Abuelita, who has always been so supportive of learning and writing for both me and my brother.

Joseph Bridges
Thanks to my wife Amber. Dealing with me is a challenge on a daily basis and I am grateful for everything you do for me and how you support me.

To my son Nathan who will probably never know a world without Facebook I hope you take advantage of this medium throughout your life.

Thanks to Dad for your support and ear and mom for making James and me take typing class.

Table of Contents

Chapter 1 – Making Money on Facebook Without Having To Have 10,000 "Friends"

Business owners can no longer ignore Facebook. In the pages following, I am going to outline a step by step plan for business owners, entrepreneurs, and sales professionals to make money from Facebook.

This book is created for any business owner who has been searching for the answer to the question "How do I make money for my business from being on Facebook?"

Over 500 million people belong to Facebook from all across the globe. Fifty percent of these people log in on a daily basis. Picture a chance at putting your product or service in front of 250 million people on a daily basis. They are waiting to find your company, your product, your service, and tell their friends.

The market for business owners, sales professionals, and entrepreneurs is limitless with Facebook is limitless provided there is a plan to follow. If you are a company of just one or you have employees with a storefront, the pages that follow outline a plan for you to make money on Facebook. You will discover methods, tactics, & strategies that will guide you to generate sales for your business in a very cost-effective, reliable, and systematic way.

Todd Bates, Entrepreneur, & Business Coach

For the last 20 years I have helped over 20,000 small business owners build businesses. Personally, I have built 47 different companies that market different products or services to different niches.

Throughout this book my co-authors and I are going to reveal how to make money with Facebook. My main website where you can get additional resources on marketing, sales conversion, and business strategy can be found at www.ToddBatesSystems.com and I would invite you to visit that website in-between chapters.

Along with my co-authors, we annually conduct over 200 seminars, workshops, and meetings for small business owners across the country. I have been doing these live training workshops for the last 20 years. There is nothing like working with entrepreneurs needing to grow their businesses. One day we look forward to meeting you at one of our live events.

For the last several years, more and more questions have come from my attendees, clients, and partners about Facebook. At these live events, business owners frequently ask me the following questions:

- How do I make money from being on Facebook?

- How do I avoid the chit chat and "white noise"?

- How do I make sure this is a system for my business and not a total waste of time?

These questions are valid questions. Business owners, sales professionals, and entrepreneurs don't have time to invest their energy or hard earned effort in something that isn't going to generate sales and results.

What This Facebook Training Book Will Do For You

This book is going to give you a systematic method for making money on Facebook. The detail that I am going to provide to you in the following pages will allow you to have a very profitable Facebook machine.

The goal of this book is to provide you an additional profit center in your business. Even if you have tried Facebook previously, I would like to invite you to continue reading to discover how to make money from what you are doing. A business can always get more money in less time from what they are doing and I promise to give you a plan to do just that on Facebook.

How To Have The Mindset That Will Make You Money On Facebook

When a business owner wants to make money on Facebook, the first question that I ask them is the following:

"What is the purpose of Facebook?"

Most business owners answer the above question in the following way:

- "To network"

- "To connect with my clients"

- "To be seen by prospects"

While all of the above may be true, the goal of Facebook for a business is to get more leads. I have a mantra that I encourage all of my clients to adopt and I would encourage you to do the same. The mantra is the following:

"Leads solve everything!"

Most businesses need more chances.

Many business owners are on Facebook, yet very few ever see any sales from their efforts. Let's look at the mindset that business owners need to adopt when they want to make Facebook a system that generates sales.

Understanding The Different Markets For Your Business On Facebook

Facebook provides a wonderful opportunity for businesses when they realize the potential for their business and with whom they are communicating.

The first market that I want to reveal to you for your business on Facebook is reconnecting with your database. You may have their e-mail address, mailing address, and even their direct phone number, yet I want you to find them on Facebook.

There are people, as strange as it may seem who don't

check their e-mail daily, yet they won't go an hour without logging onto Facebook. Connecting with your current database on Facebook is another way to keep them in your world.

A second market on Facebook that I find the most interesting from a marketing perspective is those that don't know you. Facebook is a place where a business can find brand new, qualified, and able clients to purchase their product or service. The key is to be able to find these people in a systematic way. A business owner has to be able to find these new prospects without wasting their precious time and hard earned money.

A business owner that realizes they can generate more sales from their current clients and those that don't yet know them will be able to increase their business quickly and cost effectively.

8 Rules For Business Owners To Generate Sales From Facebook

A trait of entrepreneurs is that they struggle to stay focused on one task. What I have discovered over the last 20 years of helping entrepreneurs is that when I give my clients a set of rules to follow, they follow them.

Entrepreneurs love their freedom of choice yet they love to have successful businesses the most. One of the ways that entrepreneurs can have both is having a set of rules to follow when implementing a new system in their business.

The following rules will provide you with the needed structure to implement the rest of the system that I will outline for you in this book. It has taken over 18 months, thousands of hours of testing by my team, and hundreds of client reports to develop these rules.

I would encourage you to put these 8 rules in a place where you can view them on a daily basis.

Rule #1 For Facebook Success

This might seem obvious considering what I have covered so far; however Rule #1 is this:

Focus on Leads

This isn't a contest on how many people you can get to visit you on Facebook, tell you that they know you, or that they have seen you on Facebook.

Making money on Facebook is about generating leads for your business. It is about building a system where your business can systematically connect with prospects, current clients, and future clients, not once, but multiple times.

Anything else that happens for your business such as branding, fame, or goodwill is great, yet not the focus that will lead to money for your company.

Rule #2 A Deeper Connection With Your Database

Your business is sitting on gold right now. There is cash in your database waiting to jump into your pocket if you can just find it. You may have e-mail addresses, phone numbers, and even mailing addresses.

What you are probably missing right now is a connection with your prospects on Facebook. Fifty percent of Facebook's population logs on daily. Your current customers want to hear from you where they love to spend their free time.

While your prospects are catching up on what's happening with their friends, you will be able to reach them to further connect with your company.

At first, building a deeper relationship with your database may seem like an overwhelming task. Allow me to provide you with a few more rules that will help relieve any anxiety you might have.

Regardless of the size of your database, I am only going to ask you to connect with the top 25%. The top 25% of your database contains the individuals who are going to refer you and buy additional products or services from your company.

This rule is called the 75/25 rule. 75% of your database is, for the most part, a waste of time. They may do something eventually, however spending time, energy, and effort on them will not generate a return like spending time on the top 25%.

Allow me to give you an example of this rule in action. At one of my seminars, an attendee said to me "Todd, I have a database of 40,000 and I can't possible connect with all of them on Facebook." I asked him on the next break to check on where his sales were coming from for his company.

The majority of his sales for his company came from 9,000 individuals or 22.5% of his database. This was not a surprise to me!

Rule #3 Interact More Consistently With All Potential Clients For Your Company

Interacting with prospects is a guaranteed way to generate more sales through your business. Anytime a business owner talks with more prospects, e-mails prospects, and meets with more prospects, more sales are generated.

The question then is why don't business owners do these activities?

99% of entrepreneurs suffer from E.I.D, Entrepreneurial Idiot Disease. It is a disease that prevents business owners from doing the necessary tasks for success on a daily basis. I cover it in detail in the book "E.I.D - Entrepreneurial Idiot Disease, 6 Steps to a 7 Figure Net Income".

Interaction on Facebook for success comes down to having the focus on the money making communication. Communicating with your potential clients on Facebook using direct messages, Facebook events, photos, videos, and interest-piquing updates generates consistent sales when done without fail.

The key to consistency is removing yourself from the equation. When these activities can be done automatically or take mere minutes to do, the business owner has time to get them done.

Later in this book I will reveal to you how to automate virtually all of your marketing on Facebook, or reduce it down to minutes on a daily basis. When a task is easy, takes little time, and enjoyable, the business owner will overcome their E.I.D and perform the task.

Rule #4 Time Management For $$$ On Facebook

The biggest excuse that business owners, sales professionals, and entrepreneurs provide for not getting their business on Facebook is the time it takes. They talk about the time to set it up, the time to maintain it, and yes, even the time to follow-up on the leads from Facebook.

To illustrate, my team had outlined a step by step plan of attack for a client. We provided a 6 Step Plan along with this book. After reviewing the plan, the client said the following:

"When all these prospects start to respond to this information, how will I have time?"

A business owner should always have time to speak to prospects who are interested in their product or service. My goal with the rules of time management on Facebook is to help you avoid what we call "Facebookitis". "Facebookitis" is where you look at your watch at 9:00 am and the next thing you realize it is noon and you haven't done anything other than be on Facebook.

To prevent the disease, there are three rules of time management for generating sales on Facebook.

Rule #1 Of Facebook Time Management
15 Minutes Maximum Spent on Facebook Lead Generation on a Daily Basis Monday Through Friday

Chatting with prospects about their weekend is fine to do in your spare time. The goal here is to generate a profit from your activities.

This rule cannot be broken. You might be thinking to yourself, "There is so much to be done on Facebook, how can I get it all done?" Rest assured, the following chapters in this book will reveal those details to you.

For now, the rule I need you to adopt is that spending more than 15 minutes daily on Facebook will only result in reduced profits for your business.

Rule #2 Of Facebook Time Management
15 minutes of time, energy, and effort on Facebook shall produce 5 valuable conversations for your business

The more conversations you generate for your business the great the sales for your company.

Does each one of these conversations have to be done manually by you?

Business owners and entrepreneurs tend to look try and do too many tasks themselves. An assistant, part time help, or even an outside company can easily handle the conversations for you.

Rule #3 Of Facebook Time Management
5 conversations will generate 1 solid lead for your business on a daily basis

Every lead doesn't work out to a sale. Focusing on the best of the best leads is what increases productivity for a business. Finding the top leads is about having conversations to find out who is serious about your product or service and who is not ready today.

The 15-5-1 Rule For Facebook Time Management To Guarantee Facebook Will Generate Sales For Your Business

The system for success on Facebook is very simple. I am going to ask you to write down the 15-5-1 rule. This stands for 15 minutes daily to generate 5 conversations that generate 1 solid lead for your business.

You might be thinking to yourself, "My business is different" or "I don't sell over the phone or face to face."

First, every business needs leads, so no business is different from that standpoint. Selling over the phone or face to face isn't required for success on Facebook. When you don't sell face to face or over the phone, the 15 minutes becomes even more important. Through all of these steps that are going to be outlined in this book, think AUTOMATION.

You can automate follow-up, updates, even conversations to a certain degree, until intervention is needed at the point of sale.

Rule #5 For Mindset About Facebook Leads: Quantity vs. Quality

As soon as social networking came on the scene and the concept of having "friends" appeared, there was a rush to get as many friends as possible. The "get friends" approach quickly turned into taking anyone regardless of whether they would be a fit for your product or service.

Having 1,000's of friends doesn't mean you will be putting cash in your business on a daily basis. There are plenty of businesses on Facebook with 10,000 people who "Like" their business who aren't making significant income.

In a recent conversation with a client, he was bemoaning the fact that he had acquired 5,000 individuals who indicated they "Liked" his business on Facebook. The concept of "Like" on Facebook is similar to following an individual on Twitter or providing an e-mail address on a website. You are, in essence, voting for the business to succeed in some manner.

The issue the client had with his Fans is that they weren't buying anything and had no real interest in his business. He really took the shotgun approach to attracting prospects on Facebook. He had never defined what his criteria were for acquiring Fans.

Before you start diving in to attracting new prospects on Facebook, I would encourage you to ask several questions about to whom your business works best.

Three questions that every business should ask themselves before they begin to target users on Facebook are as follows:

- What age range are the top 20% of the clients

who buy from me now?

- What kind of activities are they interested in out side of my product or service?

- Where are they located geographically?

The answers to the above 3 questions will begin to build your "Target Client's Facebook Profile".

On Facebook, start to think of the quality of the prospect over the quantity. Several of the case studies included in this book have businesses where they have hundreds (not thousands) associated with their business on Facebook. These individuals regularly receive orders from their presence on Facebook and some make 6 figures annually.

Bottom line it is the quality over the quantity. When you get your quality identified you can move to adding more of the same quality.

Rule #6 For Success, How Depending on Yourself is a Disaster

Depending on yourself is the American way. Entrepreneurs are constantly heading into the world of business with the attitude "No one does it better than me and I can do it."

Believing in yourself is great and in the end you probably are the best at what you do. The issue is saving yourself from yourself. I call this disease, E.I.D, or Entrepreneurial Idiot Disease. I talk about this disease in detail in my book, <u>E.I.D - 6 Steps to a 7 Figure Net</u>

<u>Income</u>, and reveal how entrepreneurs must overcome 6 steps to get to the next level. For Facebook, the issue for entrepreneurs comes down to consistency and persistency.

In today's world of the Internet, affordable help can be found on dozens of websites. Automating 90% of the money-making tasks on Facebook can be done easily. Much of the automation can be done with affordable software or part time assistance. For now, adopting the mindset of "I have to save myself from myself" is the important part of this rule.

Rule #7 Facebook Success: Every Business MUST Find a Way To Be Interesting

A user on Facebook is looking at hundreds, if not thousands, of pieces of information. 99% of the information they see is completely useless and boring. They are scanning their News Feed in a quest. What are they looking for?

They are looking, whether they admit it or not, for something eye catching. When something catches their attention, they are hooked. They are looking for something that piques their interest.

You must believe that your business is interesting!

Accounting is a perfect example of a business that many think is not interesting. From the outside, many believe that it is just "crunching numbers." How can an accountant make his/her business interesting?

When a business needs an accountant, they are looking

for many different traits. One item that every business shares in common is the desire to save money. On Facebook, accountants can share how they save their clients on income tax, payroll, filings, and even how they refer other specialists. The information is interesting when you are looking for an accountant.

Right now, I want you to look at how your business can be made interesting. Every business can be engaging and exciting, it is just about digging into your business and communicating the interesting information with those on Facebook.

Rule #8 For Facebook Success: Manage Your Fear

Many entrepreneurs are unaware that there is something holding them back from reaching success. Somewhere deep down they have a fear that is holding them back.

With Facebook, there are several fears that must be overcome in order to successfully generate sales. The fears that are the most difficult to overcome for business owners on Facebook are the following:

- Fear of Technology

- Fear of Looking Stupid

- Fear of the Unknown

- Fear of What Other People Think

Fears prevent entrepreneurs from taking action. Staying in the current situation is easier than taking the necessary steps to overcome the self-limiting fear.

These fears may not seem related to making money on Facebook; however, they are a large obstacle. How to overcome these fears will be revealed later in this book.

To start making money on Facebook, the first step is going to have the "Jump In" mindset. There are two kinds of business owners. There are those that "Jump" and those that "Think". Thinkers keep thinking and never improve their business. Jumpers go all the way in and are willing to figure it out.

So let's jump all the way in to make money on Facebook.

What You Will Discover In Making Money With Facebook

Through this book you will discover how to make money with Facebook. Let's look at the journey that we are about to undertake together.

Facebook Marketing Message

Having a message on Facebook that shows your prospects in 10 seconds or less what they will get by joining you is critical to success. A marketing message must answer the question:

"Why should someone choose you and your business?"

Answering this question with a powerful message will separate you from your competition. To give you a sneak peek, the wrong answers to this question are "I am honest", "I am loyal", "People like me". Those are all true; however, customers and prospects expect to deal with honest and likeable companies and individuals.

Facebook Fan Pages

When you want to do business on Facebook, you need a business presence on Facebook. Regardless of the size of your company, be it 1 person (you) or an entire staff of employees, it starts with a Fan Page.

The what, how, and why of Fan Pages will be outlined in detail in this chapter so you can begin your journey of generating cash for your business.

Find Those That Will Buy From Your Business

Having a business on Facebook means making sure your best type of prospect finds you. If your business had the nicest office yet no one could find it, you wouldn't generate any sales.

This chapter will outline multiple sources of traffic that will bring you the customer who can actually buy from your business.

Overcoming Your Fear to Generate Sales From Facebook

We can be our own worst enemy. Overcoming our own self-limits and discovering how to manage this on a daily basis will be handled throughout this book.

Special attention will be paid to systems, methods, and techniques that allow us to automate marketing on Facebook. Through automation, you will discover that your business runs on autopilot, and you make money by staying out of your own way.

Converting Facebook Prospects To Sales For Your Business

Leads are great, however, sales are better. There are two sides of the equation when you want to make money on Facebook. There is the marketing side (having people find you) and the conversion side.

Making money on Facebook isn't about pounding your prospects into submission. There is an art and a science to converting Facebook prospects into sales for your business.

The good news is that 15% of the leads that you generate will be worth your company's time, energy, and effort. The bad news is that 85% will not be worth your effort. This is called the 85/15 formula.

Finding the 15% that will take action is not as daunting as it might seem. There is a systematic approach you will find easy to put in place that will be revealed in the conversion chapter.

A Step by Step Plan For Making Money on Facebook

By the end of this book you will have a step by step plan for making money on Facebook. Each step will give you additional skills to generate money for you and your business.

Let's jump into this adventure together.

Chapter 2 – Giving Facebook Users a Compelling Reason to "Like" You

On Facebook, the community has virtually endless choices. They are being asked to "Vote" for this, "Like" this, and add this "App". How do they decide on what they should do?

They take action on the offers that are the most irresistible. To make money for your business on Facebook, your company must have an irresistible offer. This offer must serve your niche.

Regardless of your business, there is a niche to it, whether you are selling a product like copiers, cars, or real estate. Even if you are service-based such as financial planners, medical professionals, or accountants, you have a niche and we need to find this niche in order for your business to be successful on Facebook.

When deciding on your niche on Facebook, the #1 question that has to be answered is the following:

Why should someone choose you?

This question is one that, for some reason, stumps many business owners. You can also think of it as "How am I different than my competition?"

Many entrepreneurs don't understand their true role in

their business. For example, when I ask accountants, "What is your #1 job?". They usually answer, "Accounting." Their #1 job is not accounting. It is to find more people who need their accounting services. The #1 job of any business is to find more people who need their help.

Why is this important?

Facebook has over 600 million users, and when you look like every other business on Facebook, you will get results that are average to below average if you are lucky. To comprehend the size of 600 million people, the largest stadium in college football & the third largest stadium in the world, The Big House of Michigan, holds 107,501. Six hundred million users would fill the 3rd largest stadium in the world just over 5,581 times.

We need to separate ourselves quickly from our competition so we can attract our share of the market that is available to us.

Your business can separate itself from the competition with an irresistible offer called a Marketing Message.

A Marketing Message to Eliminate Your Competition & Attract the Clients You Desire

The marketing message for your business on Facebook is the foundation for making money. Some call a marketing message an elevator pitch, a 10 second test, or a USP (Unique Selling Proposition).

Your Marketing Message must be irresistible, well crafted, and unique in comparison to your competition. After all, if you sound like your competition, your message will not be effective.

The right Marketing Message can propel your business to success while the wrong one will leave your business in survival mode for a lifetime. Survival mode is when your business needs every sale to work out in your favor. Your business is constantly "chasing" money and never gets ahead. This is not a fun place to be, so let's look into how to test your message to make sure it is powerful and will effectively generate sales for your business.

The White-Out Test For Your Facebook Marketing Message

Your company's message on Facebook may be different than the one you offer on your website, printed material, or verbally to clients. The effectiveness of a message starts with the ability to pass the White Out Test.

When evaluating your business presence on Facebook, a Fan Page, I want you to print out yours and that of your competition. This is a task we regularly perform for our clients.

Before any of us look at the material, our assistant whites out the name of the company or company logo. When someone can't tell who the Fan Page belongs to, the message doesn't pass the White Out test.

In other words, if you look, act, and sound like everyone else, there is no way to generate interest from prospects on Facebook.

A few questions that you can ask yourself about your business will allow you to pass the White Out test. The questions to ask yourself are:

- Does my message sound different than my competition?

- Does my business presence look different than my competition?

- Does my message compel someone who is even remotely interested in my product or service to take some sort of action?

The sad truth that many of us don't like to admit is that when people don't know us, and even some that do, care more about their time and money than our time and money.

When your message can demonstrate how you can help them and solve their pain, you are on your way to having a powerful Marketing Message.

There are 8 categories you can select from for a Marketing Message that will compel a prospect to take action on Facebook. Before going into the 8 categories, let's look at the 6 components to a Marketing Message for your business on Facebook.

6 Components That Every Marketing Message Must

Have On Facebook When You Want to Make Money

These 6 components will guide you toward having a powerful marketing message for your business on Facebook. By putting these pieces together you will have a unique and powerful marketing message that will separate you from your competition.

WARNING: Failure to use these 6 components in your message will result in less money in your pocket from being on Facebook.

Being Specific Is The Way To Attract Immediate Attention

The first component that your message must contain is specificity. For example, there are companies who talk about having "Fast service." What does "fast" mean? Being general on Facebook will not attract prospects to you. When your company can do something quickly, you need to let the prospect know how quickly. Can it be done in 24 hours? Can it be done in 15 minutes?

This component also works when companies talk about saving a prospect money. Nothing is more irritating than hearing "We will save you money!" How much money specifically can be saved when using your company, product, or service?

A Consistent Message On Facebook is Required ONLY When You Want to Make Money

On Facebook, users are exposed to hundreds of different updates daily just in their News Feeds. Some see thousands, depending on how many friends they have. With this kind of information overload, a business looking to make money on Facebook needs to have a consistent message.

Your message needs to show up everywhere possible on Facebook. From updates on your Fan Page, direct messages to those who like your page, notes, pictures, and even videos. As a business owner, you may be feeling like "Aren't I going to be beating them over the head with my message?" You don't have to be obnoxious about it; however consistency is key as prospects will otherwise miss out on your message.

For example, James, one of the authors of this book, provides a service where he reviews the Facebook presence for businesses. His message, that he is constantly communicating, is that he will improve the effectiveness by at least 18% or you won't pay. This message appears in videos that he does e-mails, notes, blog posts, direct messages, and even pictures.

Users on Facebook, like individuals who use the Internet, will have a medium that they prefer. Those that watch your videos may never see your updates. Consistency is the only way to guarantee your prospects will see your message.

Facebook Users Will Pay More When There Is a Higher Perceived Value Associated With Your Product or Service

There are products or services that are virtually the

same product that customers will pay substantially more for. A company that does this well and has a large presence on Facebook is Toyota.

The luxury division of Toyota is Lexus. Lexus makes several sedans, however, one sedan that Lexus makes shares a number of components as the top end Toyota sedan, the Toyota Avalon. The cars aren't identical; however, they share a large number of parts and systems.

A buyer of a Lexus will pay substantially more for the Lexus equivalent. In some cases they are paying 30% more for a similar vehicle. The Lexus has a high perceived value that the customer is more than willing to pay.

How can you increase the perceived value of your product or service to your future customers?

The Modern Economy Of Facebook is About Making Everything As Risk Free As Possible

A relationship for a business on Facebook begins when they can get a prospect to "Like" their page. We will discuss pages in detail later, however, the question that your page must answer is "How risk free is it to join my company by clicking 'Like'?"

There has to be a reason for a prospect to click "Like" on your page. The more your message can demonstrate that it is risk free to join your company, the more prospects you will attract.

Risk Takers Will Be Rewarded On Facebook While Those Who Play It Safe Will Lose...Badly

There is risk in every business. For a business, the safer their message is on Facebook, the riskier it is to their bottom line.

When the goal is to generate sales for your business on Facebook, you have to take a risk with the message. Desperate companies and desperate people take risks. A business that pushes the envelope with their message will be rewarded.

No One Likes To Stay Home On Saturday Night When All The Cool Kids Are At a Party

When your business jumps all the way in to Facebook, you will discover that there is a party happening. Business can be done at a party, and it is your company's job to attract as many people as possible from this party to do business now and in the future with your company.

Your message needs to make a prospect feel that they are joining a party that they just can't miss out on. When they look at your message, they have to feel that by not clicking "Like" they are passing on an opportunity to be at the party where all of the cool kids are going to be.

Keep in mind that a well done message and Fan Page will convert upward of 50% of visitors to join your party. Let them know that they will be missing out on all the action. The only way they can get into the party and see what's happening is to simply click "Like".

It will be the best party that they ever attended provided they click "Like", so let them know they are missing out when they don't take immediate action.

8 Marketing Message Categories That Will Have Facebook Prospects Joining Your Company's Conversation

Users on Facebook are exposed to 1,000's of messages on a daily basis. Attracting their attention is your #1 goal with your marketing message. After you have their attention you can turn them into a customer for your business.

You are going to find 8 marketing message categories and examples of how to use them in this section. The goal in this process is to find one that you put all over your business presence on Facebook.

On Facebook, the most effective marketing is "interrupt" marketing. This means that we are trying to break the user's concentration from checking in on their friends and attract them to your company instead. The message has to be extremely powerful in order to accomplish this goal.

You will notice that these categories and messages will cause your business to look extremely different from others on Facebook. When your business is different, it will generate sales Let's look at the categories of marketing messages so you can find the one that fits your business.

Using $$$ To Differentiate Your Company On Facebook From The Competition

Many business owners look to compete on "the lowest price". While this can work, it can also turn your business into a commodity or put you in a price war with your competition.

Using the "lowest" price isn't the only way to use money as a marketing message. A few questions that you can ask yourself about your business are the following:

- Do you offer additional methods to pay? Ex. Can people use a layaway or break up payments?

- Do you have a version of your product or service that can be offered for less than your competition?

- How much do they save by using your product or service?

- Can they finance their purchase with you?

When working with price, the key is to offer prospects three options. You may lead with the one that is the lowest price; however, having only that option will have you stuck in survival mode.

Let's cover an example of how you can use price to your advantage and then use it with options.

One of the businesses that we have is creating Fan Pages for business owners. With our company, you can get a Fan Page for several hundred dollars; however, it is a basic version. Many are attracted to the message and the product so they investigate further.

After researching the options with the company, many business owners decide they want a more customized version of a Fan Page as well as additional services. We first attract them with the message about price; however, they often choose another option after further investigation.

Additional questions to consider when using this message are as follows:

- Do I have a specific product or service that people love that would attract massive ATTENTION at a certain price?

- How flexible can I be in how I take payment?

- What is a customer worth to my business in the long term?

The last question is an important one. For most businesses, they do great with referrals. Getting a client the first time is the hard part of the equation. Losing money on sales isn't any option for most companies unless they are extremely large companies.

For most businesses, if you can break even on the customer on a particular product or service, your business will grow because of referrals and up sells.

When looking at this category, look at all of the options

your business has available.

Letting Facebook Users Know "How" Your Quality Is Superior

At the end of the day, customers want to purchase a product or service that will last. They want to know that they are purchasing a quality product. You can't just say "We produce quality products" , because customers already expect this.

Facebook users are visual users, so they need to see quickly how your product or service is higher than your competition.

An example of a high quality product in a niche industry is Deering Banjos. They are manufacturers of exactly what you would think, banjos. You can purchase a banjo for as little as $399 to over $10,000.

What is interesting about Deering Banjos is their use of quality products regardless of the price of the banjo. For example, in their entry level banjo, the materials are still hand select by the owner and the process is 100% American made. Prospects can see this quality on their Facebook presence through pictures and even comments by their own customers. Images and video are an instant method to communicate the quality difference in your product.

This category also works for service-based industries as well. A recent client operated a niche consulting business. They provided a selection of services to small business owners in a geographic area.

As happens in the world of consulting, clients asked for services that this business didn't provide. It presented the client with an opportunity to refer additional business as well as differentiate the referrals that the client was receiving.

For this client, he put every referral through a 3 step qualification process. Every referral that the client received was pre-qualified by the consultant, provided at least 3 references, and was audited after every transaction.

The consultant was able to advertise to his clients and prospects that he performed additional services that virtually guaranteed the quality of the referral that they were receiving.

A few questions to ask yourself to effectively use the quality marketing message category for your business on Facebook are:

- How much better (specifically) is the quality of your product?

- Do you perform services that are of a higher quality than your competition?

- How is the quality of your product different than those in your industry?

Communicating the answers to these questions with video, audio, & images on Facebook to your prospects will separate you quickly from your competition.

Letting Facebook Prospects Know How Many Extras They Will Get With Your Company

Facebook users, like the rest of us, want additional services or products for the same amount of money.

Extras that your competition normally charges for will provide you the most impact with your prospects. In many industries, there are customary charges that 99% of the industry charges for. The key to making extras work in a marketing message with Facebook users, is that they must have a high perceived value.

As an example, a client has a small web development company. The company offers solutions tailored to specific industries. In the web development industry, virtually 100% of companies charge to host the website. Prices range from $9.95 monthly to $100 and up.

He decided to offer an extra service by offering FREE hosting for 12 months. The free hosting was a value of over $240 to the prospect, wasn't offered by any of his competitors, and had a high perceived value by prospects.

Everyone loves a little something extra, and on Facebook, providing users with a visual of what they can expect to get by joining your company is key. Several questions that you can ask yourself when using the extra category of marketing message are as follows:

- What item costs you very little, yet people love?

- What does your competition charge for that

you can give away for FREE or next to free, (ex, $1), for your customers?

- How can you shout this extra to prospects on Facebook?

Offering extras is a great way to generate sales without lowering prices. Prospects want more, so give them more and your competition won't know what hit them.

How to Use Your Communication As a Marketing Message On Facebook

This category is for service-based companies. Facebook users, like many of us who use the Internet, are tired of making requests, phone calls, and inquiries to companies only to have them never returned.

For a company to be able to use communication as a marketing message your prospects need to know immediately how you are different than your competition. There are four methods of communication that will attract attention your way. You can compete on phone, e-mail, direct mail, & social communication.

We are in an instant world and the more responsive your company is, the more over the top your communication can be with your customers and prospects.

The answers to the following three questions will help you build a message around communication with your prospects.

- How fast do you answer requests? Is it in minutes?

- Can your future prospects see how you answer your questions in real time?

- What kind of answers do prospects get? Ex. Do they get answers via text, Twitter, video, direct Facebook message, etc.?

Facebook provides a terrific opportunity to communicate in real time with your prospects' questions. A Dinner Theatre client (See the case study section of the book) demonstrates how to use the Wall to generate current sales and future sales.

For the Dinner Theatre company, they are always working on selling the next show. They frequently get questions such as "Are there group discounts?", "How long is the event?", "How many tickets are left?" etc. Customers and prospects get to see these questions answered in real time on the Facebook wall.

Communication works well when you demonstrate how fast, effective, and efficient your communication is with your prospects. When possible, keep your communication or resolutions public so your future prospects can see how you quickly, efficiently, and effectively handle requests. Public communication will create the proof for your message.

Providing Facebook Users With the Proof They Demand to Use Your Services

The burden of proof for companies has always existed, however, the Internet and especially social networking websites like Facebook, have changed the game of proof for every company.

You might be thinking to yourself, "I am a brand new company. How do I provide proof of my product or service when it is new?" The first sale, as many have said, can be the toughest. Selling a product or service to a friend, or even giving it away to a friend to get a testimonial, is well worth the validity it creates.

One client wanted to start a website business for local businesses. While this is not a "totally new idea", there is always room for one more when you have marketing and determination. Instead of creating dozens of templates for people to see that might never get used, we had this client go out and volunteer to do a website for his church.

The church was in need of a website, was happy to have one built, and even paid for the work. Whatever your product or service is, having proof before you hit the market is always preferred.

Facebook provides a unique opportunity for proof that will generate sales for your business. Let's look into the details of providing proof for your Facebook prospects to see what will compel them to buy.

Each of the methods described below can be used. It is best to start off with one of the categories below and add to them over time.

Facebook Users Love Audio Testimonials

The power of audio will never go away. There is something about hearing someone else talk about a product or service that you are considering that makes it easier to purchase.

There are tools that allow you to put an MP3 file on any website, however with Facebook, you can reference a simple MP3 just about anywhere and it instantly becomes available to those who "Like" your page. A past client can be the one to actually sell your product or service for you. What better sales person can be found?

Audio testimonials should address objections and concerns that prospects have when considering your product or service. It can be helpful to write down the top 10 objections to your product or service. As you encounter clients who overcame these objections to become clients, they can record testimonials for future use.

Video is Facebook Gold For Testimonials

Facebook users love video. Whatever your thoughts are about video right now, the best thing to do is set those aside. The best way to think about video is like having a walking, talking, raving Fan 24/7 working on behalf of your company.

One of the obstacles with video is the perception that it is difficult to obtain. Video can now be easily obtained with a camera that costs less than $150.00. These cameras are easy to use and even easier to get the video onto your computer for a quick upload.

Fan Pages even have a separate tab that you can dedicate to video. In the Resources section of this book, we provide additional tips on how to effectively use video for conversion for your business on Facebook.

Using The Written Word To Sell Your Products

Written testimonials have always been powerful. Over the years, unscrupulous marketers have abused written testimonials and "faked" them. Written testimonials can be turned into PDF, or even images, and referenced on Facebook in order to verify their authenticity.

For one client, we had them turn 117 letters they had from past and present clients into images. This process was quite easy and turned their "old" testimonials into "new" powerful testimonials they could use to generate sales on Facebook.

Success Stories That Can't Be Faked

To make proof effective it must be as real as possible. For certain types of Fan Pages, a review tab is readily available. This is a tab where users can leave feedback about your company's product or service.

The reviews show the profile picture of the Facebook user who left the profile. One can also quickly click to visit that user's profile. For anyone who has ever used the website, LinkedIn, this feature should seem very familiar.

Facebook users must take the time to fill out the review on your page knowing that others will be able to trace the review back to them. These reviews are valuable and should be added to your regular cycle of proof.

Statistics To Compel Your Facebook Prospects To Take Action

The old saying goes "torture numbers and they will confess to anything." With this being true, finding a number to "torture" for your business is critical for the category of statistics to be effective.

This category isn't about lying; it is about finding one truthful statistic that your company does better than your competition. One key statistic that demonstrates how clearly your product or service can help solve your prospects' pain. This will get them to take action.

You might be thinking to yourself, "What kind of statistic could I have?". An insurance agent who is a client discovered, through research, that she saved clients on average $356 a year. This stat was a very real, concrete, and relevant fact to her target market. Her target market is, of course, anyone looking to save money on their insurance.

Let's look at how you can put statistics to work on your behalf.

To make statistics work as a marketing message, we need to start with research to reveal the needed information.

- Find the industry averages for your product or service. This is generally available through trade associations or through Internet research.

- Look at the past 4-6 months worth of transactions you have had that you feel your company does the best. You probably already have an idea of what your company does the best; however, the key is to find the real numbers.

Once you know your company's numbers against your industry or competition, you will be able to come up with a killer statistic. The statistic may be in the form of a percentage, dollar amount, or number.

Regardless of what your statistic is, the more over the top it is the more effective it will be. It is recommended to keep the research that you perform in case you are asked to verify your statistic at a later date.

As an example, a CPA performed the following research. He compared his clients' taxes before he worked with them to after his work was finished. He discovered that he saved clients an average of $896.56. He saved all of the records in case he was asked about how he arrived at this number by future clients.

Regardless of whether you choose to use statistics as your primary marketing message, it is recommended to have at least one killer statistic at your disposal. Prospects love them and you can always use this compelling data in future communication with your prospects.

Letting Facebook Prospects Know They Are Getting a Team

Do you have a team of people ready, willing, and able to help your clients?

Even having part time help means you have a team ready to help your clients. Everybody wants more, especially when they don't have to pay for it. This marketing message is about letting your prospects know how much help they are really getting.

As an example, Doctor's offices have staff. One doctor client has 12 staff members to help him service clients. He has nurses, receptionists, booker keepers, office managers, and even janitorial staff to make sure his office is clean and well kept.

Most people only look at selecting "the Doctor." They don't even look at the entire experience. On his Facebook presence, his entire staff is clearly visible in pictures, video, and audio. Testimonials, as mentioned in previous marketing categories, even mention the staff and not the Doctor.

For this category to be effective, look at everyone who helps your business. You may have a part time book keeper, financial planner, cleaning staff, and even family that helps your business.

Including these individuals as part of your team makes this marketing message category effective to users on

Facebook.

Guarantee The Success Of Your Product or Service To Users On Facebook

The more risk free you can make your product or service, the more sales you will generate for your business. Many companies fear putting out guarantees because they can't imagine living up to the expectations.

This is the most powerful category of all marketing messages. Even if this isn't your primary marketing message, finding something your business can guarantee will increase your sales and frighten your competition.

In using guarantees, the key to success is the following mantra:

"The Farther You Are Willing To Go With A Guarantee, The More Money You Will Make"

For example, a client, referenced in the Case Study section of this book, has a lawn care business. Lawn care is a tough business and competition is everywhere.

In their business, they provide a 100% Lawn Satisfaction Guarantee or their clients don't pay for the service. This guarantee is clearly and easily readable from their Facebook Fan Page. When you have a guarantee, make sure everyone knows about it.

This lawn care business is located in the state of Texas.

Think about this guarantee for just a moment. Texas can get really hot, cold, end everything in between. Many lawn care owners wouldn't provide this guarantee out of fear. They would fear losing the service for that month.

When a company performs well, what does it have to fear?

There will always be clients who are unhappy even without a guarantee. Wouldn't you like more business because you were willing to guarantee your service?

For this category, there are several questions to ask yourself about your company's product or service.

- What do my customers hate about my industry?

- What could I guarantee if I had to guarantee something?

- How over the top am I willing to be with my guarantee?

With guarantees, one key component is making sure the customer has to follow at least a simple set of criteria. For example, a client who sells physical products in the automotive industry, uses the criteria that the part can't have been previously used. The product can be opened, no box with it, even be missing the receipt, it just can't be used in order for the customer to get 100% of their money back.

In this day and age, there is no excuse for not having a

guarantee. Guarantees will make you money; however, failure to have one will cost you money.

Facebook Marketing Message Action Plan

Knowing the marketing categories that are available to you to generate business on Facebook is one thing, and taking action is another.

To make a marketing message work on Facebook there are 3 steps to take.

1. Review the 8 marketing message categories that have been covered in this chapter.

2. Pick 1 marketing message category to hang your hat on. One of them will resonate with you and your company's products or service.

3. Develop a marketing message to use on your Facebook Fan Page and make sure it is instantly viewable when a prospect lands on your page.

Chapter 3 - Overcoming Your Facebook Fears to Start Making Money Now

Fears can be crippling. They can not only prevent our success, they can prevent us from even trying to succeed. If you don't overcome your fears, the ones that are really holding you back, then you have no chance of making money.

This holds true for most areas of business. Fears, especially those dealing with technology, will most certainly prevent you from putting into action a powerful Facebook system. I want you to understand that all of us have fear. The key to success isn't to simply "get over it" or "deal with it". The key to succeeding with fear is to understand it, manage it, and then conquer it. This process of fear management will allow you to unleash the power of Facebook. It will keep your sales growing and keep your competition scared to compete.

Fear is one of those subjects that most adults don't want to admit to. They feel it's a feeling that only children suffer from. Most often, I only get those who attend my live events who are bold enough to acknowledge their fear. People come up to me and say "I do have the fear of technology or the fear of what to do." They usually stand there and hope I am going to say that they just need to go out there and "do it".

Most people feel that a trial and error approach is the way to get over it.

The "overcome" approach just doesn't work for 99% of people. It takes too long and is filled with too much pain. For most of us, we need a detailed plan of attack to overcome our fears.

In this chapter I will identify the fears that my clients have run into. I will point out the fears that have been shared with me from my one on one clients. I will even share with you the fears that I have battled myself.

First, we will deal with fear management, then how to solve it. After that, we will deal with what the reality is, and how to get through it once and for all. Fear is not just a single item to address. We will dive into five areas of fear that I have identified after studying over 20,000 clients.

The fears we will explore, identify, and manage on the way to success are:

- Fear of technology

- Fear of looking stupid

- Fear of what other people think of you

- Fear of being overwhelmed

- Fear of success

Oddly enough, I can share with you that over all of those who have attended my events, the number one fear is, beyond a doubt, the fear of success. It creeps its way into thoughts, actions, and can be absolutely crippling.

We are going to break each of these fears down in detail. You might relate only to one, and then again, you might relate to more. Be honest with yourself. This might not initially feel like it is directly related to Facebook; however, it's the number one item that can prevent you from taking your business to the next level.

Fear #1 - Fear of Technology

As Facebook is an online platform for marketing, I wanted to address this one first. When I first share about Facebook, this fear really stops business owners. They know they want growth, they can see a huge untapped potential for sales, but they just shut down. They think they have to understand more about computers. One of the more common responses I hear is "When I figure out how it works, then, I can do the marketing". For some reason most people get trapped by the thinking that they have to know how it all works before they can use it.

Before I share more on how to beat the fear of technology, I want you to think of your car. Do you understand how every part of your car works? I mean literally, everything from the moment you turn the key in your ignition, to what happens when you press the pedal to the floor. Do you understand how every part provides that benefit of great transportation?

My guess is probably not, but you get in daily to drive your car, right? You don't have to understand every aspect of something to get the most out of it.

Now, before understanding more about Facebook, I want you to think in terms of "What help do you need?" What specific help will get you to the next level?

A client came to me and shared that she liked my Facebook approach. The fundamentals made sense. Then she started telling me that she didn't know how to do pictures, wasn't sure about doing updates, creating events, etc. After she rattled off a few other items, I asked her to tell me specifically what she DID know and specifically what she DIDN'T know. I told her to go through some of my online tutorials and then come back to me.

After just a week, she came back to me and shared that she was OK doing some of the basic tasks now. She shared she still wasn't comfortable doing events or working with her new Fan Page, though. She invested just a small amount of time to determine WHAT the few items were for which she really needed help. Her list was much smaller than the first time she came to me. You will be able to relieve quite a bit of anxiety when you don't confuse the process and can get clear on what you need.

When you understand what is needed, you will be on the right path. I want you to understand your next step on a deep, deep level. Whether you need help with videos, doing updates, notes, etc doesn't really matter. Understand that the skill you may need doesn't have to come from you.

Some of my clients suffer from what I have named Entrepreneurial Idiot Disease. They think they have to do and master everything themselves. Some of them, before getting on a call with me, would actually try to go and sign up for a degree in computers, just to work on Facebook. Trying to do everything yourself isn't reasonable and it just won't work.

Getting trapped in this thinking can lead to an affliction that I call "When/Then Disease". I see it in some of the attendees of my seminars. They come up to me with a saying like "Todd, when I learn technology, then I will do X" or "When I have time, then I will do X." Should you get too tough of a case of "When/Then Disease", you might not ever get your Facebook marketing to the level that you deserve.

The final part to solving the fear of technology is to understand where you can get help. The internet can often be too big of a resource to look for help, so I want to point you in the right direction. Go to Guru.com or Elance.com. These websites are filled with people who can help you improve your business. You can get people to do something as simple as find addresses of local businesses to put my Facebook marketing methods into action. With just a few minutes of investment, you can post work and receive 10, 20, and even upwards of 30 proposals of eager and talented people that will happily do the work for you. Some tasks you can have done will cost you as little as $25.

To help you see how I have battled the fear of technology in my own business, I want to share a quick story. At the time of writing this book, I have 47 different businesses. That means I have 47 different websites, products, etc. Even with all of these websites running I only have two employees. Using the power of Elance.com and Guru.com, I have found 20 different contractors who continue to help, but they only do so on a contract basis. You can find people who can do any part of your business on these sites, and you can find the help fast.

Fear #2 - Fear of Looking Stupid

I asked someone at one of my seminars a point blank question. This gentleman had been participating all day, but I could feel he wasn't really jumping all the way in. I simply asked him, "Why wouldn't you jump into Facebook?" With 500+ million people, your friends, co-workers, family members, your competition, and knowing there is an opportunity to make money, why don't you get involved?

Compared to his previous answers that day, this one was the most honest. He simply stated "I don't want to look stupid."

It's a fear that prevents many people from public speaking too. The fear of looking stupid can prevent us from trying new marketing, new technologies, and many other great opportunities.

The first solution to this fear I would like to share with you is one that may even sound counter intuitive. I invite you to consider that being vulnerable to those who know you, your database and those who don't know you will attract people to you. It will attract people to you in waves! People far too often try to put up a shield of invincibility, and that's false. By sharing your vulnerabilities, people will embrace you and you will find more support than any false bravado could provide.

Solution two to the fear of looking stupid is to take a risk. Yes, jump out of the "box" that you have become too accustomed to. Be bold, and people will appreciate that you have the courage to take a risk (I have found most people simply "wish" they could take more risks).

I had a client who was up there in years. She was up enough in years that I called her "Grandma". At one of my events, she listened patiently, but she was resistant to the idea that Facebook could help her. She said she was just too far "over the hill" and that Facebook was for young people. She didn't feel there was a match for what she wanted to do with the community on Facebook.

Her product served a unique niche that I felt she could tap into with the millions of conversations happening daily. I invited her to take a risk and put it out there. Although she initially approached it with a little hesitation, she put her product out there with 100% action. When she did that, her family, friends, and others who knew her were absolutely thrilled! She had an overwhelmingly positive response from everyone she came into contact with. She sold more of her product, generated more leads, and she did all of it because she took a risk and was willing to expose her vulnerabilities.

When you are willing to share that you are vulnerable, it actually attracts people to you. At one of my seminars I held on public speaking, I shared this concept with the audience. I asked one of my audience members, "Why do you think I have such great rapport at my events?"

People gave me a variety of answers. They shared statements like "Todd it's because you have done 2,200+ events" or "Todd, it's because you must spend time preparing." Not even close.

The reason I have great conversion, and great rapport with my audiences, is because I make myself vulnerable and I am not afraid of taking a risk. I tell everyone that I have been broker, that I have been $75,000+ in debt several times, and that I got a stunning 1.7 GPA in college. I share that I have suffered from Entrepreneurial Idiot Disease.

I let the entire audience know that I am just like them. I am in the same boat right along with them and that allows them to connect with me.

Far too often people have this perception of what people think about them. What YOU think and what they actually think can be two entirely different things. My point is that people may already think you are stupid. I am joking of course, but my point is to stop worrying about looking stupid, expose your vulnerabilities, and take a risk. That leads me to the next fear, the fear of what other people think of you.

Fear #3 - Fear of What Other People Think Of You

There is a simple solution to this fear. Understand the following at a very minute level. Even your close friends, your past clients, those around you, and those who "love" you, want you to remain at your current level of success.

At their core, they want you to maintain at a level of success they feel comfortable with to keep you where you are. They fear you leaving them because you are more successful. Even your friends and relatives want you to remain at their level of success because they don't manage their fear.

I remember 15 years ago with one of my first

coaches. I asked him about some of the marketing that he was helping me put into action. It was over the top, way out of the box, and I just wasn't that comfortable with it. I asked him, "What do you think my clients think of me?" His answer was shockingly simple, "They don't. They don't think of you, they are worried about themselves, worried about their own lives; they aren't worried about what you are doing."

It hit my ego, but I knew he was right. In our minds, we have the perception that people think of us much more than they really do. When you understand how little you cross the minds of others, it frees you from being controlled by the fear of what other people think of you.

Truly, I want you to embrace this idea. If you want to be loved by everyone, then be average, be normal. Being average is not what this is all about. If you want a powerful Facebook system, then I am going to ask you to be different. Not just a little different, so different that you feel you can't even find the box that you jumped out of.

Examine my 95/5. This rule means that only 5% of the people you bring into your world on Facebook will you want to bring further into yours. It may sound like a tough "numbers game", but the numbers don't lie. There will only be 5% of people with which you would actually enjoy spending time. To make the point perfectly clear, I would invite you to envision that this number of people is so elite, it is the number with which you would actually want to have dinner.

Quoting a famous line from the movie Jerry Maguire, "It's not show friends, it's show business." Getting over this fear requires you to grow up, create a system, over come your fears, and jump all the way in. It simply won't work until you jump all the way in.

Fear #4 - Fear of Being Overwhelmed

Don't let the anticipation of a huge volume of leads and business prevent you from starting. Understand that implementing a powerful Facebook marketing system is a process. You don't put it into action overnight. Each step of the way in the system, you will be able to embrace a new level of success; pace yourself.

It's going to take 30,60,90+ days to put this system into action. You won't be flooded with 1,000's of leads in just a few hours right off the bat. This is 15 minutes a day of work to making it a system. This is a powerful, cheap, and quick system to generate leads with more people. It is not overwhelming.

There is one simple fact that I would invite you to embrace when it comes to fears. The simple fact is, 95% of all the fears that you feel, face, or jump into your head never come true! You are worrying for NO reason at all. Entrepreneurial Idiot Disease (E.I.D) means you feel the pain of the fear before the reality even hits you.

Just think about that. Ninety five percent of your fears won't come true, not ever. You know this in your own world. Fear management comes down to ignoring what you are thinking. Ignore that chatter box in your head. You will be amazed at how just a small amount of ignoring those negative thoughts in your head will prevent you from being trapped by the fear of being overwhelmed.

Fear #5 - Fear of Success

The first question I would ask you to see if you suffer from this fear is quite simply "Do your clients like you?"

You would likely share with me that, yes, people like you. They love you, they love your service, and they enjoy everything you have done. It goes even deeper because you would likely share with me that you understand your clients; you know their challenges and can name any detail about them.

That's not your problem. The problem is you haven't been able to get more clients because of the fear of success. You might have questions jumping into your thoughts like:

What If I do get more business?

What if my income does jump dramatically?

Would I not be able to see my family?

Would I spend 900 hours a week at my job?

Would I have to give up my vacation plans?

These are questions I ask of people at seminars and boot camps all the time. I can physically see audience members shut down when I start to ask them about the fear of success. They get uncomfortable because they think more success is more time working, more success is more headaches, and more success is more problems.

The first solution to the fear of success is to challenge yourself with a question. I want you to ask yourself if it is easier to do more or less business. Before you continue to read on, I want you to answer that question for yourself.

Now, with that answer firmly planted in your mind, I want to share with you the following. It's easier to do MORE business.

Why?

Before I share how more business is easier, I want you to think about the situation of trying to have success with less business. With less business, there is more stress. You have to do every part of your business, you have to count on every sale, and should one sale not come through, it could spell disaster.

With more business, you are in a different situation. You can outsource the tasks that don't make the most money. You can get help to grow your business. You get to be the Dr. in your business.

Here is what I mean by being the Dr. in your business. In the Doctor's office, who makes more money, the Doctor or the head nurse?

The Doctor of course!

More importantly, though, does the Doctor do the majority of the work?

No! The Doctor comes in with each patient for just a few minutes, does only the highest dollar hour work, and moves on to the next patient.

The Doctor can do that because he has focused on more business, not less. He has made it a point to have a constant flow of patients, focus on only the high dollar an hour work, and outsource the rest of the work. By concentrating on more business, you get to be the Doctor, and you can move past the fear of success.

The second solution I would invite you to consider to overcome the fear of success, is to identify three successful people in different aspects of life. I had one of my clients do this activity. She wanted to find someone who was a great example of being healthy. She wanted to find someone who was a model in working out. She went to her network, and she actually found someone who was an actual model. This person shared with her what she ate, how she worked out, and the price she paid to stay healthy. Connecting with this model, she was able to get her health in order.

I invite you to consider doing this same activity in three categories of life. Identify someone in spiritual success, health, finance, etc. The categories aren't important, just identify three categories that are important to you and people that you can ask two questions. The two questions that I would suggest you ask them are:

How did you do it?

Was it worth it?

Was it worth it to be in great shape? Was it worth it to have a great relationship? Was it worth it to have 20 million in the bank instead of being broke? It doesn't matter the category, just find three people and ask them the questions. Take time to listen and apply it to your life to overcome the fear of success.

The third solution to overcoming the fear of success is to picture yourself right now. Picture yourself generating more leads, dealing with more income, and being happier.

Now, ask yourself if that vision is worth it. Or, do you want to be where you are at With worrying, constant fear, constant agony, and feeling overwhelmed. Picture yourself where you want to be.

Identifying Your Biggest Fear

The bottom line that I want to make clear to you in this chapter is that you won't be able to have success on Facebook without identifying your biggest fear. It is essential to have a specific plan of attack and then manage your fear daily. Not just sometimes, not just when you feel fear creeping in; manage your fear daily. The strange part about fear is that it doesn't go away because you conquer it once. Those who reach the levels of success that they truly deserve are those that manage it daily.

I was sharing with one of my clients about a party I recently went to in my neighborhood. Now, in my neighborhood, homes cost a few million dollars. Most of the people in my neighborhood are relatively successful financially. They have a few million in the bank. Many of them are small business owners and entrepreneurs. One of the surprising statements I hear is a complaint that they have to "grind it out" every single day. Yes, even with a few million in the bank, their complaint is about having the opportunity to work.

For example, one of my neighbors owns a few sporting good stores. He has owned these stores for over 15 years. He has done very well, continues to do well, and is worth a few million dollars. His main complaint to me is that he works daily.

It brings me to the point that those who have success MAKE themselves do what others won't do daily.

If you don't have a solution to overcome your fear, and a step-by-step fear management plan in place, your Facebook presence won't work. You might put it into action for a few weeks, but then you will flush it because you haven't properly managed your fear.

As you finish this chapter, I invite you to be brutally honest with yourself. Write down your biggest fear and use the solutions here to manage your fear daily. The greater your level of honesty with yourself, the faster you will hit the level of success that you envision.

Chapter 4 - Discover How Your Fan Page Can Be the Foundation to Generating Leads, Sales, and Building Your Brand

You have now seen that marketing on Facebook is more than considering your friend count. It's not about having to be friendly, playing games, taking quizzes, or playing an endless amount of videos. There are those who waste time on social networking, but as a business owner, your goals are different.

You understand that there is a mindset to being on Facebook for business. The mindset to marketing for success on Facebook is about generating leads, generating referrals, and pushing your message to make it absolutely irresistible for people not to take action.

Having success on Facebook doesn't mean you have to be technical. It doesn't even mean you have to be "social." One of the most important elements to success is simply overcoming your fear. You can't think too much about what you are doing with your marketing. There are those who think too much and get trapped with paralysis analysis. Those who get trapped with too much analysis never get their business to the next level. They just keep looking for new features and carefully just "consider" how it will affect their business, rather than put it into action.

What I want you to consider is whether you are a jumper or a thinker. Jumpers "jump" and put marketing into action. Jumpers go feet first and put the methods and strategies that I have shared in the previous chapters into immediate action. They don't wait, they take action and their reward is more leads and sales than their competition.

Jumpers always outperform thinkers. Thinkers get stuck in trying to figure out "why" they should do something. They compare their business to their competition; they read endless case studies, create spreadsheets, and while they are doing that, their business suffers. Thinkers get stuck in what I refer to as "paralysis by analysis." The endless planning leads to just more endless planning.

In many of the corporate clients that I coach, I try to quickly get them out of this "thinking" behavior. They want to schedule meetings, form committees, and run the ideas by the "stakeholders." In the meantime, their smaller competition is gaining market share. The newcomer on the block is stealing their sales volume. Too many meetings and too much analysis can lead you to the poor house, regardless of the size your company is today.

In social networking, many business owners, entrepreneurs, and sales professionals get trapped by trying to determine what social networking is "all about." They try to review case studies, look at trends, read newspaper articles, and then they don't put any strategy into action.

As you move from being trapped by thinking into action mode, I invite you to consider that one key component to your success on Facebook is your marketing message. Whether you are selling a product or service isn't important. To pique interest and cut through the chatter on the social networks, you can't look like everyone else. Looking like everyone else won't get your business noticed and it certainly won't generate sales daily. With your marketing message in place, (It should be based on saving people time and money) you will nearly have the foundation of your Facebook marketing system complete.

A Foundation Built for Success on Facebook

The foundation of a building can keep it standing for 100's of years. Look at some of the oldest buildings, like the famed Coliseum. It has been standing for almost 2,000 years because it has a powerful foundation. Sure, the walls may have deteriorated a bit, but it still stands proudly with 1,000's and 1,000's of people visiting annually.

Even with all of the environmental changes, the foundation of the coliseum remains strong. New building techniques? They have absolutely evolved, and yet those didn't need to be applied to the stadium, because it was originally built to last.

Why do I mention this now? Business changes quickly. Facebook changes at seemingly the speed of light with new applications, new policies, and new users. Changes are inevitable, but with a strong foundation, you will have success regardless of what occurs.

Your foundation for success is composed of three elements. Get these elements correct and it doesn't matter what the latest changes to the Newsfeed will be. Your foundation will allow you to weather the storm and make easy adaptations.

Mindset

The mindset of the business owner on Facebook is different than 99% of the other users. Remember, your mindset is one that focuses on adding value, not endless chatter. A Doctor doesn't care if the patient that comes in is her "friend". She understands that she is the expert, she provides value, and that patient is lucky to be able to get in to see her. Your mindset of Facebook can't be any different than a top Doctor when you want to make money.

Overcoming Fears

Fear management is one of the top reasons entrepreneurs have success or fail. With technology like Facebook, it can take quite a bit of fear management to have success. Whether you have fear of the unknown, fear of technology, fear of rejection, or any other fear, managing your fear is what will allow you to break free and generate business through this massive social network.

Your Marketing Message

Your marketing message is the last part of your foundation and is crucial. Consider it the cornerstone of your foundation. A powerful marketing message separates you from your competition. It compels prospects to take action, and it makes it irresistible for people to resist working with you. The more interest-piquing and provocative your message becomes, the more people will rush to your business and the more they will want to share it with their friends.

A foundation is great, but the Romans didn't have massive sporting events on just a foundation. The goal is to generate more leads and more business. In order to obtain this goal, we need a Fan Page.

Your Fan Page is Your House

With your foundation firmly in place, it is time to build a powerful house. On Facebook, your house is your Fan Page. Your house, when built correctly, will handle not just a few "Friends," but thousands and thousands of friends. More importantly, you can build these friendships into people who are absolute Fanatics about your business.

These Fanatics will happily tell others about your business. They will scream from their seats about the excellence of your product or service. Take care of them, and your business will thrive. Be careful not to hurt these Fans, as that undying loyalty can be your worst enemy. More on that later.

In a nutshell, your Fan Page is like a website within Facebook. It's crucial to the success of your business; however, most business owners are taking the wrong approach. Throughout this chapter, I will share with you how to avoid common problems, how to get your Fan Page producing, and how you can create one that generates Fans that will turn into leads for your business. When you complete the rules that I will share with you, you will quickly soar to the top, and your competition will be left scratching their heads.

> **WARNING**: *A strong word of caution as you proceed. Although a Fan Page is similar to a web page, I would discourage you from recreating your website within Facebook. The conversation happening on the social networks is different. They are looking for a different way to have their interest piqued. Get lazy and just "copy" your website into Facebook, and you will be disappointed with the results. You could fall into the trap of saying "Facebook doesn't work" and miss out on the opportunity of a 500+ million person audience.*

Key Elements To Success

Before diving into the rules of success with a Fan Page, it's worth noting why Facebook has had such tremendous success. Unlike other social networks which throw businesses and individuals all together, Facebook has made a clear definition of where businesses can be found and where you can network to connect with friends and family.

I call this the two sides of Facebook. There is the personal side, and the business side. When thinking of the personal side, I invite you to think of a cocktail party. At a cocktail party, you can do business, right? Of course you can! The right parties can open the doors to business deals with millions of dollars, only when you know the rules.

For example, envision yourself at a black tie party. Cars are being parked by the valet; everyone is dressed in their most stunning attire. As you network among the crowd, do you speak only of business? Do you ask each person how they can help you? I hope not! Should you have that approach, you will certainly be unpopular and it's likely you will be spiking the punch bowl to have fun.

That's the challenge with only using the personal side of Facebook. You can't share too much business or you risk getting kicked out! Yes, Facebook can and will kick you out of their site should you do too much marketing or solicitation from your personal profile. They want their network to remain somewhat personal. They don't want it to be a spam fest of offers like other networks have transformed into.

From a marketing perspective, we want to direct as many people as possible to our business Fan Page. Our Fan Page allows us to be as direct and interest-piquing as we want, and it can be all related to business.

The goal for our Fan Page is to get as many new people as possible, get more conversations, add more value, and get more people interested in what we have to offer. When you differentiate yourself from everyone else, you will quickly separate yourself from the competition. The greater your difference, the more you will look like the expert.

Why Most People NEVER Get It To Work

If marketing on Facebook were easy, everyone would get it to work. There wouldn't be a need for countless articles, blogs, or even books to be written because it would be so obvious. Many people are trying, yet few have cracked the code to dominate their niche. I have found that there are two big reasons that prevent most people from succeeding with their marketing.

Blind Marketing

Blind marketing can be frustrating and most people in this category don't even realize that they are literally headed east looking for a sunset. The business owners, sales professionals, and entrepreneurs in this category simply don't know what to do. They are unsure of what steps they should take. They might try a Facebook Ad, they might even start a group or page, but they always just put their toe in the water. Unfortunately, they are so unsure of "what" to do, that they get trapped by doing nothing.

Fortunately, those who are blind to marketing on Facebook can be healed. When the steps are revealed to them, they can quickly hit the ground running and achieve success. Don't be alarmed if you feel this applies to you, as you are just pages away from seeing the light.

Hope Marketing

Hope Marketing is when you go full steam ahead, but you have built the wrong house. You blaze a path ahead and just "hope" it works out. This usually happens when people attempt to do their marketing from their personal profile. They figure it might save them a little bit of money and time. Besides the personal profile is the most familiar making it appear easier.

Unfortunately, when you do marketing from your personal profile, you run into a few major problems. The first challenge is that you can't do geographic marketing. Facebook allows you to target users in specific cities, states, etc, but NOT when you are using your personal profile. The second big challenge, when you are trapped by Hope Marketing, is that you can't track what those you are connected to are really engaged with. In other words, you don't know if they play your videos, you don't know if they are checking out all of the pictures you are sharing, you can't even tell what days are the most popular for delivering interactions!

You literally can only "hope" it works because you will have no metrics on what is working or not working. Take for example one of my clients.

She called me regarding her marketing efforts on Facebook. She shared with me that she had just over 350 people on her personal profile. She was off to a good start, at least on the personal side of social networking. She wanted to know why she wasn't generating much business, as she was pretty proud of being connected to over 350 new people in just 40 days.

I proceeded to ask her the following questions:

- Where are they located?

- What days do they interact with your content the most?

- What links have been most popular?

- What types of media do they like the best? Video? Photos? Audio?

Unfortunately, she couldn't answer any of the questions. She had worked diligently to build up a list of new Friends but she couldn't share the information with me that would get her closer to making money.

Her 350 people weren't doing much good because she didn't know about them. Marketing 101 Lesson: The more you know about your prospects, the EASIER it is to target them. The less you know, the more you are doing BLIND and HOPE Marketing.

This just brings to mind a classic marketing lesson that is worth review. All too often I get my clients calling me after they have sent a direct mail piece. They choose a bad list, they market with the wrong offer, they send the wrong medium and then they come back to me with a question like "Why did my direct mail piece fail?" What I am saying is that the methods I am sharing about Facebook marketing is the same thing. Unless you have a Fan Page, you won't be able to have success on Facebook because you won't be attacking with the right information or medium.

Your Fan Page Solution Should Follow 7 Key Rules When You Want It To Succeed

Most people put a Fan Page into action with little thought. They look at graphics; figure they should put their logo on it, and viola, they're done! With this approach, there is little chance for success. Remember, a Fan Page is basically a website within Facebook. I say basically because it makes the most sense, but don't run out now and try to recreate your existing website as a Fan Page.

Before I share with you the seven rules, I want to put your mind at ease. It is likely you are already on Facebook and are connected to 100+ friends (the average user is connected to 130). These will eventually be the first people that you invite to your Fan Page once it's created. I have found that about 20% of the people that my clients are connected to personally can help them generate more business. The other 80%, like that nice cousin in Iowa, are unlikely to help your business get to the next level.

Rule #1: Your Marketing Message

Your marketing message needs to be unique. It should clearly be spelled out on your Fan Page and be blatantly obvious to anyone who lands there. Preferably, it addresses the aspects of time and money. Your message will be a success when you can click at it and quickly answer the question of "Why would someone click 'like'?" If you can't answer that question, then go back to the drawing board and create another message.

Most business owners simply try to reuse a slogan or a catch phrase. Those won't do any good on any marketing piece, and they fail miserably on Facebook. When your marketing message piques interest, then you will have people rushing to you for help.

Rule #2: Demonstrate Your Business Personlity

People on Facebook are having conversations daily. They are using chat, they are making comments, and they are involved in different groups. Tap into the power of those conversations! You can't create a blah, vanilla Fan Page and expect them to want to talk about it.

Let them see what your personality is like, how you can save them time, and how by connecting they can save money. It should be obvious that by taking a few seconds to click "Like," they will get valuable information. You are already helpful in your business, so make sure your Fan Page carefully reveals how they would be missing out if they didn't take the leap to connect.

Rule #3: Geographically Target Your Fan Page

In a world where the internet makes it easy to get information from all over the world, I am going to challenge you to have the vision of attacking a local market. With the addition of new features like Facebook Places, geo-targeting your Fan Page can bring massive results for businesses that have a local presence (i.e. restaurants, retail stores, insurance agencies, etc).

Having a local aspect to your Fan Page can have dramatically different results. For example, I have 47 different websites. Each website has a different niche, serves a different market, etc. When I take one of my websites, like my Denver Marketing Coach website, I can get more conversations and more leads because I appear as a local expert. People want to know they can reach out and connect with someone who truly understands their market.

Do whatever you can to make this part of your Fan Page and watch how many local prospects you connect with.

Rule #4: Graphically Appealing

Your Fan Page needs to be designed by someone who understands Facebook. I had someone at one of my seminars say, "Well, any graphic designer can design one." That would be like saying anyone can drive a race car! Sure, we all know how to drive, but do we know how to get the real performance out of a Formula 1 racecar? Hardly!

In order for a Fan Page to have success, it needs to be designed by a graphic designer who understands the conversation that is occurring on Facebook. It can't look like a template. It can't have just a basic "change this color" or "write text here" type of look and feel. When your page looks like everyone else's, you won't get the desired results. Templates may save time, but they won't end up making you money.

Let me be clear. There are very key parts to each design. There should be an element that draws their attention to the "Like" button. There should be an aspect that compliments your existing branding. The images should be rich and convey your subject matter (i.e. If you are selling real estate, you might want to have a home on your Fan Page).

In the example, you can get an idea of what a Fan Page can look like. This is a Fan Page that my team created for one of our clients.   You can quickly see how attention is drawn with an arrow, how their guarantee is revealed, and how the graphics reveal the quality of work they provide.

Rule #5: Video

You absolutely need to have video shared through your Fan Page. It doesn't have to be on your landing tab, but video needs to be part of your Fan Page. Don't go crazy and think that you need to get expensive equipment or you need to learn some Fancy editing software.

Video can be cheap and it can be very simple. You can record simple short videos in front of the camera sharing about your product or service. You can shoot video from behind the camera of happy customers or of an upcoming product you are going to release. Those who take the leap into sharing video will be ahead of their competition quickly, as most people still have too many fears about putting it into action.

Before you think that you can't put this rule into action, I want you to consider how many people watch television. Now I want you to consider how many people are on YouTube (current count is over 73 million). Do you think with as much TV and millions of users on YouTube, that video provides a natural interaction? Give your next customer what they crave!

Rule #6: Audio

You might think that audio is only reserved for musicians and bands that are jumping on Facebook, but it's not so! Audio can be easily shared through your Fan Page, and it has the added benefit, much like video, of drawing people to stay on your page while they play it.

Don't get stumped by what you might share, just consider the following. What would your prospects want to hear from you? What would people find valuable? What is a common conversation that you have with prospects before they buy? What is a fear that you overcome in a 1 on 1 conversation that you could share with everyone?

Answer a few of those questions and you will have what you need to create audio for your Fan Page.

Rule #7: The 10 Second Rule

The goal of a Fan Page is to get them to click "Like". You can refer to them as a "Fan" or someone who "Likes" your business, but the bottom line is, you need them to click "Like." With this rule, we need to get a total stranger to click "Like" within the first 10 seconds of them landing on the page.

You don't have long to grab someone's attention; I would say 10 seconds max. People are constantly being bombarded with new offers, new media, and when you can cut through that confusion, you can get a prospect. The moment they take that small amount of time investment and click that tiny button, is the moment we get someone new to connect. After that small click, you get the opportunity to add value, pique interest, build rapport and get them to take action with your business! It all starts with that simple first click.

I can't stress the importance of the moment they click "Like". I had one client who shared with me that he had 2,000 people hit his Fan Page in 1 week! A great number for sure. When I asked him how many new Fans he had gained, he said 20.

"Twenty?" I asked.

Out of 2,000 people, he only had 20 people who took the opportunity to want more information by clicking "Like." After a quick look at his page, I shared with him that his call to action wasn't obvious, it looked too much like a template, and he wasn't drawing the user's attention to the "Like" button. His conversion was far too low, and that means he wasn't able to take advantage of all of those great people who hit his page. Don't let his mistake happen to you; take time to ensure you follow the rules.

Consider This As We Are Building Your House on Facebook

What I shared here in this chapter are the core methods to having a powerful Fan Page presence on Facebook. These rules have come from testing and implementation of Fan Pages with over 2,000 clients.

I have a team of people who create these pages for businesses. They don't miss a single rule; in fact, they helped develop the rules. I have graphic designers, Facebook developers, web developers, my lead "web nerds," and copy writers just to create a single Fan Page. The reason I have this entire team of people is we create 100's of new Fan Pages for my clients all year long.

It isn't an easy process. Facebook makes changes constantly, and we adapt to those changes and adapt the marketing strategies to remain competitive. It's hard work; really, if it was easy EVERYONE would already have a successful Fan Page.

When you want to discover more on how we can help you with your Fan Page, you can visit me at www.ToddBatesSystems.com/FanPages, or you can see how I put the methods into action, live, with my Fan Page at www.Facebook.com/ToddBatesSystems. Don't freak out! Each Fan Page is different, each one is unique, but each one follows the core rules that I shared here.

> **Tech Tip**: When you want to see who I call my "web nerds" in action, you can find them on Facebook as well at www.Facebook.com/FanPageSystem .

If you don't have a great house, if it's not appealing, if it doesn't have your personality, and doesn't have a great marketing message, then it simply won't work. That's why I have a team of people to put these together. If it was simple, any template would do.

I would challenge you not to put the other methods in this book into action without first getting your house built.

Chapter 5 – Turning Friends, Fans, & Those Who Know You on Facebook into Sales for Your Business

With any system of marketing, there are two parts. No matter what type of marketing you put into action, it always boils down to just two elements. At times, we, as business owners, try to make marketing more complex. We can get stuck in endless planning and that prevents us from success.

To help you eliminate the need for meetings and planning, I invite you to consider that two key parts to your marketing system are:

Getting people To Take Notice

This means getting prospects to take notice of your marketing. Grabbing the attention of people who are busy and piquing their interest with your advertising efforts.

Conversion

When you get attention (whether that's a phone call, email, etc.) it is essential to convert them from a prospect to a client. On Facebook, this means getting the Friends that are connected to your business to take action.

Most marketing and advertising professionals only want to talk about getting people to take notice. They want to wow you with dazzling graphics, Fancy websites, and talk about how to create a "community" of people. If you asked them about how you can make money from that attention, it is likely they would change the subject.

Driving traffic and getting attention is fun. It's the sexy part of marketing; however, I am going to challenge your thoughts in this chapter. In this chapter I will share with you how to get people to have an exchange. I will share with you how you can take simple interactions as your opportunity to transform prospects into customers.

Before I share with you key methods to successful conversion on Facebook, I will expose the bad methods. I will uncover the normal, bad, and unprofitable approaches that most entrepreneurs mistakenly put into action. After exposing these poor practices, I will outline the path to conversion mastery.

The 5 Biggest Mistakes Business Owners Make on Facebook

Even though marketing on the social networks is relatively new compared to other mediums, there has been no shortage of mistakes. The challenges of a massive new type of application, freedom to do almost anything, and "gurus" who give poor advice, have led many business owners down the path of wasting 100's of hours of work and thousands of dollars.

#1 - Looking Like A Sales Person

The first problem most business owners make is looking like a sales person. They create a presence that talks only about them. They create status updates that share features of their product or service. They even get all of their graphics created around their "brand."

The reality is that people don't like sales people. They don't want products or services to be "pitched" at them. They don't want to feel high pressure, like walking onto a used car lot. People want fun, and you can convert that fun into money for your business when you don't look like a sales person.

#2 Lack of Consistency

Remember the rule we shared of working on your social marketing 15 minutes a day? It's a small investment of time and yet most business owners don't put it into action. Just consider for a moment how you would feel when 15 minutes a day (5 days a week) added 2, 3, or even 10 more sales monthly?

Would that be worth a small time investment?

Tragically, many business owners who jump on to Facebook don't hold themselves accountable to a schedule. They don't stick with a level of consistency that generates success. Just 15 minutes a day, with the right activities in place, is a simple formula that most just won't follow.

#3 Talking About Themselves

Facebook, Twitter, and even LinkedIn have been created around conversation. Much of the conversation that occurs is useless gibberish. As businesses have jumped on, many have fallen into the trap of regurgitating this useless dribble. They think talking about their business or talking about themselves will bring them business.

Remember, people don't care about you. People care about themselves. They care about their time, their money and their interests. When the conversation that you put into action is about yourself, you get ignored. You get lost in the "white noise" of the News Feed and might think that it doesn't work.

#4 Vague Statements

Sharing vague statements about your product or service will leave you wondering why no one is taking action. A cheesy slogan or motto can just be thrown away, unless you have the money to launch nationwide commercials.

You better have a clear and specific marketing message. For example, if you shared something like "I will save you time and money," it doesn't provide any real benefit. It's too vague. How much time can you save them? How much money?

#5 Suffering from E.I.D

E.I.D stands for Entrepreneurial Idiot Disease. When you are plagued with E.I.D., you constantly start new projects, you have many different ideas you have put into action at the 80% level, and you might even be stuck in survival mode.

When you don't manage your E.I.D. on a daily basis, you won't have the consistency to make your Facebook marketing system work for you. You won't stick with the 15 minutes a day of money making activities.

People get frustrated when they don't get fast results. They lose motivation. They stop taking action after two weeks. These are all symptoms of the disease. It's usually at the two week mark that people call us and complain. They share their frustration that they haven't seen massive results.

For those clients who have worked with us in the past, we usually share an over the top question with them like "Oh my gosh, you aren't a multi-millionaire after two weeks?"! It's at that moment they realize they need to buckle down and keep working the system.

Keys to Success for Conversion

Now that you know what to avoid, we want to share with you the keys to success. Most people get stuck in the mistakes we shared earlier. They get trapped constantly heading east looking for a sunset. By knowing what to avoid, you will be ahead of your competition. By knowing what works and putting it into action, you will be able to generate sales daily.

Some of the keys to conversion we will share with you will be very different from what you have read anywhere else. They might sound odd, and they might challenge the "norm" of what you have been led to believe. We want to challenge your thoughts now and ask, do you make more money by looking like everyone else or being different?

In the keys to conversion, we will share methods that

will allow you to look different. The more you are different and stand out, the more interest you pique, the more money you will make.

#1 Biggest Key to Conversion – Interest-piquing Updates

That little text box that cleverly reads "What's on your mind?" This open ended question by Facebook has left many business owners stumped, and others to share useless dribble. It's one of the most powerful and easy ways to get conversion, yet most people put little effort into crafting updates. Just because it takes a few minutes to share something, don't underestimate its power.

Most of the client updates we review, prior to working with them, are boring. The updates aren't interesting, and they don't share anything that would grab attention. One set of updates that we reviewed for a client were the following:

I just had coffee this morning, a great way to start the day.

I am having a sale today at my store, come on by.

You get the point right. Who cares? Who cares about her having coffee? Why should they come by for the sale? These updates didn't attract attention and were too focused on her and her business.

A better approach that we would suggest is to be different to get results. We would encourage you to use what we refer to as interest-piquing questions as your updates. They are never statements; they pique interest by using specific benefits to your prospects.

For example, we invite you to consider the following updates that you could use as your status updates:

Want to discover how to save 15% in the next 58 minutes? Find out now at [website link]

What loan is best for you? Discover 7 key items that most lenders won't tell you before you decide...

How do you save 18% monthly and improve business productivity by 20%? Find out today [website link]

Why do most diets really fail? Don't spend another dime on a bad diet program until you read this [website link]

As you can see from these updates, they are far more interest-piquing than most updates you read. Some of our clients get so bold as to share the exact amounts of how much they save clients. After all, how interested would you be if you could find out how someone saved their customer $1,267 dollars? It almost doesn't matter what it's about, you feel compelled to find out more.

Let's be clear. Will everyone respond to these updates?

No! That's the point. Not everyone will interact on each update. Only those who are interested and who really want to find out more will engage with you and your business. You don't want to sort through every prospect; you just want to work with those who are most interested in what you are offering.

The number one key to success with conversion on Facebook is to ask questions. The more interest-piquing, the more specific the benefits, the more business you will generate.

If it was just about doing interest-piquing updates to get results, we would see more people succeed. The reality is that the updates only work when they are put into action consistently. There are many tools to help you with your consistency. The great part about these tools is that most can be used for free.

Two tools that we have found to help, both ourselves and our clients, are SocialOomph.com and Futuretweets.com. Both of these tools give you the power to schedule out your interest-piquing updates.

No longer do you have to remember to login daily and write something that is interest-piquing. Now you can sit down one time and input updates that will be released over the next few days, weeks, or even months!

Remember, one of the key reasons that many business owners fail at marketing their business on Facebook is a lack of consistency. They don't stick to the simple schedule we outlined of daily conversions and 15 minutes a day of action. Most business owners suffer from E.I.D, they lack the consistency, and they quit too soon. Even worse, they let getting "busy" prevent them from keeping their marketing going.

The point is to get conversion. It is essential to ask

questions, be consistent, and make sure your updates are interest-piquing.

Use All of the Tools of Conversion Available To You

Just imagine there is a blank lot where a new home is to be built. This nice lot is across from your house, so you can see all of the activity. One morning, you see a contractor show up in his work truck. His truck is completely empty. When he exits his truck, he only has a hammer with him. How well do you think that home would be built if he only used a hammer? Would it even be livable?

A contractor couldn't build a home with just a hammer. He would use all of the tools he has available to build a great house. Just like that contractor will dig using an arsenal of tools, so will you to get the most conversion. Text updates are just one element of conversion. Using just text would be like that contractor just using a hammer.

Here, we want to share with you the different conversion mediums available to you within Facebook. These conversion methods can be put into action through your business Fan Page.   While pages continue to grow in the ways they can interact with prospects (through Facebook Applications) we invite you to consider the methods we share here first. After exhaustive testing, well over 2,000 hours worth, these are what we have found to help you get results fast.

Notes

Notes are a secret weapon that is unique to Facebook. You won't find this feature available on LinkedIn, Twitter, or MySpace. A note is a cross-between a status update and a blog post. It's this unique positioning that gives it its power.

Many business owners never use them, and as a result, they are leaving business on the table. To get the most out of Notes, we invite you to consider the following rules for success.

- **Note Length** – Don't go crazy writing a Note; remember it's not a blog post. The most effective Notes, those that pique interest, are between 70-150 words. You can write that in just a few minutes.

- **Format Your Note** – Facebook allows you to use bold, italics, and even bullet points. Format your Note to make it easy for your Fans and Friends to see what is most important. Don't go overkill; just draw attention to key items.

- **Headline** – Getting your Note to spread through the News Feed means making it interesting. Just like the front page of the Los Angeles Times on a Sunday, your headline better grab attention. Take an extra minute to craft a powerful headline that will compel people to want to click and read more.

- **Call to Action** – What do you want them to do?

Do you want them to comment? Do you want them to share it with their friends? Do you want them to visit your website? Make just one call to action per Note. Keep people guessing, and mix up your calls to action on each Note to keep those connected to you eager to read your latest Notes.

Just like other conversion methods, Notes work best with consistency. Put them on your social networking plan to do weekly.

Videos

Some business owners still find video to be a challenge. With equipment that can be purchased for as little as $100, there really isn't an excuse not to put video into action for your business on Facebook. Right now, less than 1% of the Facebook population is putting video to work for them on a regular basis. With this level of exclusivity, you have a huge opportunity to be different and generate leads by putting it into action.

Getting video to work for your business isn't complex. There are many different styles of videos that you can record and share. You can shoot video with you behind the camera, walking through your store. You can be in front of the camera sharing a tip, you can interview a customer, you could even have people submit questions and answer them through video.

There is no limit to what you can do with video. Before you think you might have to be a major Hollywood director to get results with this conversion medium, we invite you to consider our top three rules.

- Length – Attention spans are short. Don't waste the attention you earn by putting out a boring 10 minute video. Consider sharing videos that are 2-5 minutes in length. Mix up the times and leave yourself enough time to add value and pique interest.

- Quality – No need to spend $2,000+ on a Fancy camera and set-up. You don't need to waste $1,000's on video editing software either. You can shoot video from a cheap $100 handheld camera and get results.

- Call to Action – While some videos may just build equity with your Fans and Friends, there are videos where you will want to ask people to take action. Make it clear on what action you want the person who is watching to take.

As with anything that is new, putting video to work for you on Facebook will take patience. Make video part of your social networking plan and stick with it. Those who use video consistently will be ahead of their competition as video becomes a new standard in marketing.

Audio

Audio is one of the more infrequently used conversion mediums on Facebook. Many business owners have felt it only works for bands, but that would be a big mistake not to take advantage of this tool. Audio can be put to work in many different industries, from music stores, training companies, education, marketing, sales and more. We haven't found an industry yet that couldn't benefit from putting audio to work.

With audio, the key is to provide variety. Facebook allows users to play your audio right on the page, which means you have a captive audience. Use that attention wisely! Don't have all of your audio at just one minute. If you release just short audio clips your Fans will get bored. Consider mixing up your audio recordings into different segments. You can have audio segments that are 1-3 minutes in length, 10-15 minutes, and longer training calls that are 15 minutes or more.

As some prospects ignore video, adding audio to your marketing arsenal gives you a powerful method to connect and convert.

Photos

People love photos. Sharing photos through your Fan Page gives you a unique opportunity to grab attention. Many business owners have considered this to only be a tool for those sharing family fun, but it's actually a powerful conversion method when you put it to work for your business.

When using photos for conversion, we invite you to consider at least 3 rules.

1. Image Quality – Your photos don't need to be professional. You could share an image that is chicken scratch from a napkin. It could be a

photo you took from your iPhone or digital camera. When a picture looks more "real," people will want to engage more and share it with their friends.

2. Mix it Up – Don't just share the same type of photos. We have found great results from sharing diagrams, business models, and even pictures of our happy clients. Sharing a variety of photos keeps people eager to come back for more.

3. Description – Although a picture may tell the story of 1,000 words, consider writing a description for each photo. Writing a short description provides you the opportunity to pique the interest of your Fans. Your description also displays in the News Feed! This is very valuable space and it only takes a minute to write a powerful description.

Photos are a powerful tool when used consistently. Consider having them on your social networking marketing plan as a weekly activity. As more people interact with your photos, consider increasing the number of photos you share.

Reminders on Facebook Conversion Strategies

With the methods we shared above, you will be on your way to greater conversion. Even as Facebook continues to grow and add additional ways to grab attention and convert leads, there are methods that won't change.

We have used the following conversion strategies on Facebook and in our past experiences in sales and marketing. It's likely you won't find these methods shared elsewhere; however, these will have your marketing generating more business daily.

Reverse Selling

Reverse selling means you are interviewing prospects. You aren't answering questions, you are asking them. No longer will your sale be dictated by what the client asks. You get the opportunity to control the conversation and determine if the person qualifies to work with you. Get your prospects to jump through a few hoops.

For people to get in direct contact with you, they first need to become a Fan. After becoming a Fan, they need to make a comment (interact with you in some manner) before they can get you on the phone. When you make them jump through a few hoops, your value is higher, your exclusivity is higher, and more people will be attracted to you.

Before you start thinking this is insane, we want to share with you the attitude of reverse selling and interviewing prospects. When you want more conversion, create scarcity in your offers. For example, the status update that our client used earlier:

"Want to save 15%? Find out how to save that and maybe more in the next 58 minutes [link]"

This type of update creates scarcity. It gives people a

reason to act now. It provides a time when the offer is ending! Some of our clients make the mistake of sharing statements like *"I am available 24/7"*.

Consider that level of availability. Does your Doctor say that? Does your attorney tell you that? Pick up your phone right now and try to call your doctor directly. Will you be able to get him/her on the phone? Unless your Doctor is your parent, it isn't going to happen. You will get their office or their answering service. They make it hard to get a hold of them on purpose. They are interviewing you, they are limiting your access, and yet...we still wait to get a hold of them.

Doctors manage their scarcity. Lawyers manage their scarcity. With your Facebook marketing and conversion, we want you to get better at:

- Reverse Selling

- Making Prospects Jump Through Hoops

- Limiting Offers

- Limiting Downloads (limit your special reports to just a specific amount of time)

- Scarcity of your time (make it harder to get a hold of you)

As you get better at each of these methods, you will find yourself having very different conversations. No longer will you get bothered by the endless tire kickers. No longer will you have a flooded email inbox of people just wanting "free" help. Your conversations will be limited to those who are more worthy of your time.

Real World Facebook Conversion Strategies in Action

Marketing, especially marketing on Facebook, is about testing. As more people have joined and new features have been added, we have been testing our methods constantly. In our own businesses that we operate, with over 47 different websites, and 47 different products and services, we have found the need to put new strategies into action regularly. With over 20,000 clients over the past 20 years, they practically demand that we push the edge of marketing.

Here is what we are getting at. Last year we tested over 2,800 different conversion updates through Facebook. What we discovered was that 90% failed miserably. They didn't generate a lead, a "Like", a comment, a click, nothing! Ninety percent of the updates were an absolute total failure.

The last 10% were the ones that worked. This last select group of status updates was all questions. They all provided value, all piqued interest and had success. All of the photos that worked were different and had descriptions with them. The videos that generated results were specific lengths with powerful headlines of involving saving people time and money.

We can have a great Fan Page and even a great marketing message but there has to be more. You could set up everything correctly and generate leads, but if you don't get conversion right you will be spinning your wheels. Without conversion, you might be one of the sad few who start to think "it doesn't work."

We want to challenge you today to write down what you save clients. Write down how you save them money. When you have powerful interest-piquing updates (using all mediums available to you) that's how you will be able to generate activity and get real conversion.

Facebook is a great source of business. With over 500+ million people, and growing by millions monthly, you have a huge opportunity to tap into more business. If you run it like most people, it won't work, even if it gets to a billion people. Be different, review this chapter again, get good at conversion and interest-piquing updates.

When you want the shortcut to interest-piquing updates, we invite you to check out our done for you updates. No guessing or writers block. If you can "copy + paste," you can have them working for your business in minutes. Put over 500 updates to work for your business by visiting:

www.FBSmallBusiness.com/InterestPiquingUpdates

Chapter 6 – How to Unleash A Flood Of Traffic To Your Business on Facebook

The foundation of your success has now been built or is on its way on Facebook. A great presence on Facebook will fail if no one on Facebook is able to find you. In this next section, we are going to discuss how to have an endless supply of new Facebook users rushing to find out what you have to offer.

Mindset for Generating Traffic

Before exploring the methods of traffic generation for your presence on Facebook, having the right mindset is critical. Many believe that you can just create a Facebook Fan Page and users on Facebook will just come beating down your door.

Traffic generation on Facebook is about attracting potential prospects that can eventually buy or refer you customers to your business. Wasting time, energy, and effort on attracting "just anyone" to your presence on Facebook will cost you hard earned money.

There are 3 areas of Facebook traffic that we are going to reveal. Within each of these areas, we will discuss methods to generate results.

Picking one of these areas to master first is critical to success. Eventually putting all 3 of the different traffic mechanisms into place will build you the ultimate

Facebook machine.

Personal Referral Traffic from Facebook

The first method of traffic generation for your business presence on Facebook is your personal Facebook account. Many business owners don't want to have a personal Facebook account. They feel that this will detract from their business.

Business owners are often the faces of their business. Having a personal profile allows the business owner to profit from their personality.

There are 4 methods to generate traffic from your personal page on Facebook. Let's look into each method. Be careful not to get overwhelmed with all of the information. Putting even one into place is better than putting none.

Direct Message From Your Personal Page on Facebook

Facebook "Friends" can quickly be turned into prospects for your business by sending them a direct message. Direct messages on Facebook can be thought of like e-mail. Facebook sends the user a message which appears in their Facebook account as well as forwarding to the user's e-mail.

Harnessing the power of direct messages requires accepting a few rules. The first rule of direct messaging is knowing that it will take multiple messages to reach your prospects. You don't have to repeatedly blast your friends with messages about doing business; however,

Facebook users receive large amounts of information and may miss your original message.

To make direct messages work without abusing your Fans, make sure you test your messages first. The first part of every message to test is the subject line. The subject line will dictate whether the message is even opened.

Each message should have a single goal of getting the user to visit your new Fan Page and joining you in a business conversation. With all of the methods of traffic from your personal page, it is about moving them into a business conversation.

Suggesting Your Fan Page To Your Friends

Your friends are an asset for your business. Many people try and get their friends to buy from their business. This isn't necessarily a bad thing; however, selling to your friends can create an awkward relationship when the business transaction doesn't go well.

What if you could have your friends help you grow your business without having to buy from you?

The beauty of social networking, especially Facebook, is that your friends can help you build your business without ever buying from you.

Facebook encourages you to build your business through your friends by providing you with an easy feature that will "suggest" your page to your friends.

Many believe that "I don't know enough people to make this work." The average person knows just over 100 people. The great part is that the 100 people you know also know 100 people. For the cost of $0 you can launch your business on Facebook to 10,000+ individuals just from knowing 100 people.

The important part in this step is to take the action of suggesting your Fan Page to your friends and letting them help you grow your business.

Interest-Piquing Status Updates From Personal Facebook Presence

Many individuals attempt to do business from their personal Facebook accounts. This can end badly as Facebook clearly states that doing business from your personal account is against the rules.

Your personal account can be leveraged to build your Fan Page. Most Facebook users are unaware that the field of "What's on your mind?" can be used to generate sales for their business.

While this will be covered in detail later in this book, a quick example of a typical update that users post might look as follows:

"*Heading to the office, Mondays are the worst.*"

An update like this will not build your business on Facebook. An update that will bring users from your personal side to your business side, might look like the following:

Interest-piquing Update: "*Discover how to solve the 7 cures to back pain @ [FanPage Link]*"

By following a series of updates such as the one above, your personal friends will know that you have a business presence on Facebook. This is a quick and FREE way to build your business presence on Facebook without having to spend a single dollar and without getting kicked off of Facebook.

Top 10% of Your Facebook Friends Will Move The Heard

Everyone has friends that others follow. Their friends want to be them and be associated with whatever they are doing next.

Only 10% of your friends will meet these criteria. The key is to find the 10% so you can get them to build your business for you. The best part is it isn't going to cost you any money. These 10% want access to the latest information, products, and services.

To make this strategy effective, it only takes looking through your friends and seeing who has the highest friend account.

As an example, a client recently had only 110 friends and was launching her business on Facebook with a Fan Page. In searching through her friends, she found 8 individuals that each had 2,745+ friends.

These were her heard movers, and she was able to get them to grow her business rapidly simply by sending them a personal direct message.

5 Ways For Free Traffic For Your Fan Page

Above, we mentioned how to generate traffic from your personal page to your Fan Page. By following the steps above, you will have a base of individuals who "Like" your business.

The next step is to multiply the number of individuals who know about your business and will be your future customers. There are dozens of ways to generate high quality future prospects to your Fan Page. Let's look at 6 different methods of generating FREE traffic you can turn into your next customer.

Joining Groups That Can Help You Grow Your Business

On Facebook, there are thousands of groups that are dedicated to hobbies, passions, and any topic in between. These groups have thousands of passionate individuals who are looking to dive deeper into their interests.

Your business can profit from these groups provided you find the right groups, with the right members, and communicate with them correctly.

Let's cover an example of a recent client who is a canoe builder. This client builds custom made canoes that are of the highest quality. They are completely unique and could even be customized. It might surprise some to know that there is a group about canoes on Facebook. He is part of this group; however, he was missing out on a large opportunity.

Effectively using groups isn't about finding one group. It is about finding at least 10 groups that are closely related to your product or service. In the canoe example, there are dozens of groups that have potential future clients for your product. Groups that are associated with camping, the outdoors, kayaking, and even rock climbing, are potential clients for the canoe business.

For your business, create a list of at least 10 different closely related topics. Approaching each group one at a time will provide you a steady flow of new potential clients, provided you follow three rules of Facebook Group Operation.

Rules For Success With Facebook Groups

While there are no "official" rules for operating within Facebook groups, there are rules that need to be followed in order make money from spending your valuable time on groups on Facebook.

3 Rules That Will Make Your Time on Facebook Groups Profitable

1. Introduce yourself to the head of the group. Every group has someone who founded the group. They started it, and showing them respect is the first step to take when joining a new group. Your introduction can be as simple as "Thanks for starting this group. I look forward to being a part of it." This first introduction is critical to success in the group marketing

strategy.

2. Participate first. Participation is critical to success. Facebook users join groups to dive deeper into their passions. They don't come to groups to be sold a product. Participation in a group makes you a "member" of the group. Members like to help members and participation is your first step to generating sales.

3. Don't spam the group. Group members who only post comments such as "Buy from me" will soon be kicked out of the group. Prior to posting anything related to sales, check with the group owner. By following Steps 1 and 2, the group owner will be more than happy to allow you to make an offer to the group. Spamming is never acceptable in any group. When the only update that you send to a group is to "buy" something that is considered spamming.

For groups, the key is to get started with one group. Don't get overwhelmed with approaching all of the groups on your list. Starting with one will put you on the path to success.

Cross Marketing Your New Facebook Business

Facebook is a tremendous source of traffic; however, it is just one website. The Internet is, of course, far bigger than Facebook by itself. Cross marketing is about bringing users from other channels into your business presence on Facebook.

The question to ask for cross marketing is the following:

What additional online resources do I have access to for finding new prospects to join me on Facebook?

Let's look at a few resources that you may have at your disposal.

- Company website. You may have had your company website for several years. Your current customers and most recent prospects are familiar with your website. With a small change to your website, you can attract them to your Facebook presence. Facebook allows you to use their logo to direct customers to your website. Using the Facebook logo immediately gives your company a "cool" factor, and a logo recognized by hundreds of millions of individuals.

The easiest place to start is with your current website or blog. The question to ask yourself is "What other online sources do you have access to?" What can we offer your current online customers to join you on Facebook?

E-mailing Your Current Database To Generate Facebook Success

The number of Facebook users grows on a daily basis. Many are unaware that they can find your business on Facebook. A powerful method to quickly grow your presence on Facebook is through the e-mails of your customers that you already have.

They may already be receiving e-mails from you. Inviting them to connect with your business is another way you can add value to them. Having your customers' e-mail addresses is as valuable as jewelry and should be treated with care.

To connect with your customers and prospects on Facebook via e-mail, there are 4 important rules to follow.

Four Rules for Successful E-mails To Build Your Facebook Presence

These 4 rules will generate results without having to blast your database of e-mails excessively. It may take more than one e-mail to bring your customers from your database to Facebook. Each e-mail that you send should follow these 4 rules.

1. Tell your customers what they will get by joining you on Facebook. It has to benefit them to join. Numerous companies are making the mistake of simply saying "Join us on Facebook." Why should the customer join you? This has to be clearly explained in your e-mail.

2. Have a compelling subject line. The number one reason e-mail doesn't get opened is due to a bad subject line. Make the subject line clear, compelling, and interesting so that your prospects will open it.

3. Make them a very special offer that is only

available to those who are a Fan of yours on Facebook. Everyone likes to feel special. Providing something unique only to those who are Fans of yours on Facebook will explain why they have to join you on Facebook even when you already have their e-mail address.

4. A clear call to action must exist in your e-mail. Never assume that the reader will figure out what they should do. The call to action should clearly direct the user to visit your company on Facebook and join you.

Following the rules above will make sure the e-mail that you send to your customers and prospects will bring them to your business presence on Facebook.

SEO Article Marketing For Facebook

An added benefit of having a Facebook Fan Page, is that it will increase the ability for your business to be found on Facebook.

Article marketing, when performed correctly, will increase your business on Facebook. Let's look at how to use article marketing effectively

To make articles effective for your business presence on Facebook, there are rules to follow.

- Use a proven article website to help you market. A website such as www.EzineArticles.com is a proven article marketing website. This website is FREE and will publish your articles on multiple websites.

- Consistency counts. Writing one article will not by itself generate a flood of traffic to your Facebook Fan Page. Writing articles is about consistency. Three a week is a good target for articles. If you aren't a writer, this can be outsourced and there are many writers on the Internet who would be happy to help. Keep in mind that you get what you pay for.

- Connect articles and your Fan Page. One of the goals with each article is to make sure your current Fans of your business on Facebook see your efforts. Websites such as EzineArticles.com allow you to connect their website to Facebook. This means every time you write an article, it will appear on your Facebook Fan Page.

To make your article marketing efforts effective, a professionally done Fan Page is preferred. While creating a basic Fan Page is free, it will not have the necessary elements in order to receive the full benefits of your article marketing.

Video on Your Facebook Fan Page

Video is an extremely powerful method to grow your presence on Facebook. Part of the effectiveness of video lies in that very few Facebook users put it to work on their behalf. As an example, on YouTube, a social networking and video search engine, only 1 out of 1,000 users submit videos.

So, 999 people watch what the one person has uploaded. By using video, your business can separate itself from the competition.

A fear that many business owners have with video is "What would I talk about?" By taking an educational approach to your business, finding new topics to discuss on a monthly, weekly, or even daily basis is not difficult.

Any business can do this; however, let's look at an example of an insurance agent. Insurance is a product that many would say is "boring;" however, there are many different questions about insurance that an agent can answer.

Some of the topics that an insurance agent could address in a series of videos are:

- The #1 most misunderstood feature of life insurance

- Why combining policies saves the customer money

- What questions to ask your insurance agent before you sign

Taking the common questions your prospects have about your product, or service, is a great place to start for video.

Let's look at a few rules for video that will keep your videos easy for you to do, and entertaining for your audience.

3 Rules for Effective Facebook Videos

These rules are to help you grow your business on Facebook. By their nature, business videos don't have a tendency to go viral. Viral videos, those that spread because of their content, tend to have cats dancing on computers, or someone getting hurt. Just because your video may not go viral, doesn't mean it won't generate sales for your business.

The following 3 rules can be used to produce effective videos.

1. **Be Yourself**. The worst videos are the ones when someone is trying to be something he/she is not. When shooting video, act like your customers are in front of you and have a conversation with them.

2. **Five minutes or less**. While many websites, including Facebook, allow videos in excess of 10 minutes, the majority of users will not watch for longer than 5 minutes. Keep your videos short and to the point.

3. **Don't sell in every video**. When a user knows that they are going to be sold in every video, they will stop watching them. Focus in on education for you videos, and your Fans will buy from you.

Most of all, with video, have fun and eliminate your competition by being willing to do video.

Paid Traffic on Facebook

Facebook provides businesses with the ability to reach customers with ads. At the time of the original printing of this book, advertising on Facebook for many industries is ¼ the cost of advertising on Google.

Many users are unaware that ads even exist. These ads appear on the right-hand side of user profiles in Facebook.

A business owner has the ability to target users by geographic area as well as by demographic criteria. For example, you can target users who are male agents 25-35, and located in Los Angeles.

Rules for Successful Facebook Ads

Advertising can be expensive when you make mistakes. For that reason, we are going to provide you with rules to use that will make the most out of every dollar you spend.

For ads, there are 3 main components that make the biggest impact in your success or failure.

20+ Short Sale Listings

Discover 5 powerful short sale letters that will get you 20+ short sale listings. Letters will have sellers demanding to use you!

Joseph Bridges likes this ad.

🖒 Like

Title of an Ad

The title of an ad is 25 characters including spaces. This is your chance to capture the attention of a Facebook user.

For the title, it should interrupt the users so they pay attention to your ad.

Think of the title of your ad as your first impression to make on a prospect.

A few questions that you can ask yourself with the headline are:

- What is the one message I want to communicate to my prospect?
- What item of value can I offer them?
- Do I have a winning headline from my website that people love?
- What specifically can I offer my prospects?

You get one chance to make a first impression, and your title will determine whether the prospect takes notice and reads the rest of your ad.

Picture in Your Ad

The picture in a Facebook ad is not required; however, outside of ad headline, it is the single most important aspect of your ad.

Ads can be up to 110 wide by 80 pixels tall. The pictures that prove the most effective in generating a response in our ongoing tests, use the entire height and width provided by Facebook.

Additional items to consider when selecting a picture for your ad are as follows:

- **Colorful images generated a higher response than those without color.** For example, one of our clients ran a test for an offer of an e-book. One test had a simple picture of the book, while another had a brighter image of the book. The results of the bright book were over three times from the plain book.
- **Pictures generate an increased response rate.** Pictures of men, women, children, and families worked well for our clients. The pictures didn't necessarily have to be professional; they just had to relate to the subject that was being addressed.
- **The picture needs to relate to the product.** Many have tried using a picture that is unrelated to the product to increase the response rate from the ad. A client, without our knowledge, ran an ad with a woman in a bikini. This generated a response; however, it was not related to the product. The long term result of this was a poor campaign. It may seem obvious; however, the picture needs to relate to the product or service being offered.

For pictures, we recommend having at least three ready to test for your initial offering. Pictures can be purchased from a variety of sources on the Internet.

Body of an Ad

Appointments in 3 minutes

No rejection, no memorization, just ask a series of questions that any serious buyer should answer and book appointments, guaranteed.

Joseph Bridges likes this ad.

👍 Like

135 characters of magic!

135 characters including spaces is what an advertiser gets to convey the message to the Facebook user The goal is to persuade the user to leave their friends' profiles and take a look at the offer.

The ad length is very similar to that of a Google Ad or a good old fashioned classified ad.

In the ad, Facebook requires that the sentence be grammatically correct and you can't use excessive punctuation. Each ad goes through a review process to make sure an advertiser isn't trying to "beat" the system.

We have discovered that they will quickly reject ads that don't meet their guides. This doesn't mean that you can't push the envelope a little, it just means you have to be creative.

The ad text should be compelling enough to warrant the prospect to leave their friends profile and visit your offer.

In the ad above, the headline, image, and ad text all relate to getting more appointments in a three minute time frame. This ad was for a product that my brother and I did for real estate agents.

The ad addresses how you will get results without having to memorize lengthy scripts, which is common in that industry. Everything must work together to have an effective ad that generates sales for your company.

Additional Facebook Ad Issues

What we discovered through testing is something called ad fatigue. Ads can only appear for a certain amount of time before they have been exposed to all of your potential prospects. What this means is that you have to have multiple ads ready prior to advertising, so you can quickly change directions.

Many advertisers want to test on a really big scale and generate a flood of traffic. This sounds great; however, this can quickly rob a company, your company, of hard earned capital. When testing, test on a small scale so you can make every dollar count.

The rule for advertising that we would suggest you adopt, is the 7% rule. The 7% rule states that you can spend 7% of your average deal to generate a sale. For example, if you sell a product or service that costs $100, you can spend $7 to generate that sale.

Many overspend to generate the sale, figuring they will "catch-up" at some point. Playing "catch-up" is a dangerous came. Make sure you know your numbers ahead of time.

Finding Traffic Sources for Your Business on Facebook

Throughout this chapter, you have discovered how to

generate traffic for free from your personal Facebook account to send to your business account, for free from your business account, and even a steady and reliable source of paid traffic with Facebook ads.

The traffic sources, methods, and strategies can seem overwhelming. To have the greatest amount of success with the traffic sources that have been discussed, let's look at an action plan.

- Review the FREE traffic sources from your personal Facebook account as well as from your business Fan Page.

- Select two of the methods that were discussed that you feel best fit your personality.

- Of the two methods that you selected, put one into place in 15 minutes daily for the next 14 days.

The traffic sources on Facebook that have been discussed in this chapter will provide you with a steady and reliable source of new prospects for your business. Each one of them can be turned into a system that eventually can be delegated so you aren't doing 100% of the work yourself.

Chapter 7 - A Step by Step Plan That Virtually Guarantees Your Business Will Generate Profits from Facebook

Congratulations on making it to the end of this book. You have made the journey to have a powerful Facebook marketing system. When put into action, this system will generate a consistent and steady flow of leads and sales for your business.

In this final chapter, we will summarize the 8 critical steps to ensuring that this system will generate results for your business.

1. **Step #1 - 85%/15% rule.** Eighty five percent of your contacts will not be worth your time, energy, and effort. The goal is elimination. Everything you will do is to eliminate those people who aren't going to do business with you or interact with your company.

2. **Step #2 - You suffer from E.I.D. Entrepreneurial Idiot Disease.** If you don't automate, you will be destined for failure. You have to own up to this disease. Your business/system needs to run 24/7/365 without you. Entrepreneurs all suffer from this disease. Without admitting the problem, you will never be able to grow your business.

3. **Step #3 - The right mindset. It only takes** 15 minutes a day. This is about consistency and persistency. Automation will help. There are still steps you need to take. Get in the right mindset that you need to test, especially with ads. Understand that providing your prospects with video, audio, and pictures, will reveal what works best to generate sales. The only way to find out which medium your prospects like the best is to test.

4. **Step #4 - Identify Biggest Fears**. This may not be related to social networking; however, it is critical to success. You must identify what the fear is that has been holding you back. It may be the fear of success, fear of looking stupid, fear of going broke, fear of technology, or even fear of what others think of you. The key is to identify your fear so you can begin to manage it on a daily basis.

5. **Step #5 - Create a great marketing message.** Nothing is going to work without a great message. What are you doing to save clients time and money? You must be able to specifically answer this question for your prospects. In 10 seconds or less, a prospect needs to see how your company is different.

6. **Step #6 - Facebook Fan Page**. This is about getting serious with having your business on Facebook. A graphical Facebook Fan Page is the only way you are going to make any kind of

money on Facebook. Don't settle for anything less than a professional Facebook Fan Page.

7. **Step #7 - Traffic to Your Fan Page**. A great presence on Facebook does little if no one sees it. Driving traffic to your Fan Page is about making it a system. We covered methods that were free and methods that required an investment. Each of these methods should be put into place in a step by step manner to generate leads you can turn into sales.

8. **Step #8 - Converting those prospects through interest-piquing questions.** Answer the question of "What's in it for them?" How can you ask questions of your prospects that will pique their interest? These questions should lead your prospects down a logical path of one day buying with your company.

Putting these 8 steps into action will put your company at the forefront of revenue generation with Facebook. The worst thing that you can do with what you have discovered in the previous chapters is nothing.

The next step is to start putting everything into action. You may still have questions and that is a good thing. We have put together additional resources at www.ToddBatesSystems.com. The information that you have read has come from us helping 1,000's of entrepreneurs put Facebook into place in their business.

We look forward to hearing about your success from you!

Case Studies

The following pages contain case studies of clients that we have assisted, consulted, or coached. Each client that is featured in these pages strives to push the envelope of Facebook marketing in their business.

We encourage you to visit their pages on Facebook and connect with them. Each one of them would be happy to connect with a fellow entrepreneur who is looking to grow their business through Facebook.

Case Study of Palacio in Long Beach

A client of ours operates a magazine in Long Beach, CA that is focused on adding value to the bi-lingual community within Long Beach.

The editor and publisher of this magazine, Andrea Sulsona, had several challenges that prevented her from putting together a website. A website within Facebook actually provides her more power and was faster to set-up then a traditional website.

One of her challenges was presenting the demographic data of the target client she was reaching to local advertisers. She had the statistics from the "main" magazine; however, she needed data at a local level.

By operating her Fan Page, she is able to immediately tell prospective advertisers the demographics of the client that they are reaching. Her Fan data has become a valuable sales tool for her to sell advertising.

Getting more advertising for her magazine has been only one of the benefits since launching her publication on Facebook. Her advertisers have benefited from the additional exposure as she is able to offer them advertising on her Facebook Fan Page.

As a magazine publisher, getting more subscribers is always the goal, as this drives advertising revenue. Her Fan Page has become a source of new subscribers and additional revenue for her magazine.

Sulsona's Fan Page has become a source of information for festivals, events, and businesses to communicate to those in the bi-lingual community. Taking a traditional product such as a magazine, and moving it onto Facebook, is helping her to thrive in her efforts as a publisher in the new Internet age.

You can discover more about how a magazine publisher can ditch their website and thrive at www.Facebook.com/LBPalacio.

Case Study of a Dinner Theatre

A client of ours in San Diego, CA owns and operates a dinner theatre. A unique aspect of this dinner theatre is that it doesn't own a physical location, and operates out of a hotel ballroom. Their marketing exists primarily on the Internet and relies heavily on efforts to build awareness of the events through Facebook.

For this client, keeping current Fans and prospects aware of upcoming dates is critical to the success of the business and filling shows. They actively use an Event Tab as part of their Fan Page to show the upcoming shows.

Not all of these clients' attendees to the event RSVP through Facebook. What their Fan Page provides, though, is a schedule of their upcoming events that is easy to view.

Just as important to scheduling future events by using an Event Tab, guests can check out what happened with past events. Many don't want to be "first," so demonstrating to your market what the experience is like through social proof, makes it easier for others to follow the crowd.

Each of the events for the dinner theatre takes on a different feel, even though the script may be the same (it does change from time to time). Guests can experience what it was like by viewing the past events.

When you adopt events as part of your sales model, you may find that the lasting effects warrant adding a tab to your Fan Page so users can check out the past events and make sure they don't miss out on future opportunities with your company.

See this Dinner Theatre for yourself on Facebook at http://www.facebook.com/SDDinnerDetective.

Case Study: The Story of 1 Sylvie and 100 Fans in 8 Days

Many business owners and individuals consider the task of getting to 100 Fans a daunting challenge. Even with successful businesses, they just can't seem to see why people would want to click "Like".

The first goal to getting to 100 is simply embracing the idea that you have many great customers and prospects that are happy to connect with you. Users across Facebook will rush to your Fan Page when you give them a reason and quickly share the benefits with them.

One such user who wasted no time embracing that people would want to connect with her, is a client of ours named Sylvie Beauregard. She works in the competitive field of real estate in California. While many think that agents in California have it easy in changing economic times, only the best have been able to remain in the game.

Sylvie B. recognized that relationships were an essential part of doing business in the Central Coast. She was inspired to get to 100 Fans quickly, as she wanted to reserve a great username for her Fan Page. Realizing that the best domain names were taken over 10 years ago, her goal was to reserve the username of www.Facebook.com/PasoRoblesHomes.

Although Sylvie did not have a huge network of users on her personal profile, she was determined to get her first 100 Fans and she wanted to get it done in a week.

Sylvie embraced the conversation of the social networks, and her key action items were as follows:

Direct Messages

She reached out to people directly in her network through Facebook. Instead of merely suggesting they "Like" her page, she shared with them the challenges of keeping in touch and how she wanted to do a better job. The focus of her emails was the benefits of connecting with her on her new Fan Page.

She realized that direct messages were only part of the conversation. She wanted an active community on her Fan Page, so she went to the "real world" to get more contacts.

Live Networking

Part of her weekly activities is attending business luncheons, meetings, and networking events. Normally, in conversation she would have mentioned her website; however, in the first week of her new Fan Page, at each event she now shared about her Fan Page. She engaged in the conversation of meetings and encouraged those she met with to keep the lively conversation going online.

Although Sylvie does have a blog and website, she was able to get her first 100 Fans in just 8 days by simply using the above methods. As each person joined her Fan Page, she would welcome them and even encourage them to recommend others who might be interested. She embraced the conversation that is natural on Facebook, and transformed it into a community of eager people that are willing to do business with her.

You can certainly reach out to Sylvie and find how she continues the conversation by visiting her Fan Page - www.Facebook.com/PasoRoblesHomes

Case Study of Sheryl Smith

When deciding how to build a relationship with your Fans, a critical component is to be yourself. We call this matching your marketing to your personality.

Each company has to find its own personality regardless of the size of the company. This can seem easier to do when the company is just an individual; however, it often takes experimenting with a variety of mediums to see what will work.

A client of ours is in the real estate business. To be a high producing successful real estate agent takes work, and the job comes with many challenges that are never revealed to consumers.

Sheryl Smith is a real estate agent in the Sacramento area of Northern California. Her background is one of high producing sales in a corporate environment which she has translated into a highly successful real estate career.

How did Sheryl do in her first attempt at social networking and work on Facebook?

Needless to say, she put in great effort, yet the results were not what she was expecting. The original content that she produced lacked "Sheryl." It was valuable information, yet her Fans couldn't see her in the material that was produced.

This happens with many in their first attempts at providing valuable information on Facebook.

Fortunately, there are many different methods to provide content to Fans.

Sheryl experimented with updates, blog posts, articles, and video. What she discovered is that her personality shines with video. She not only is good with video, she also enjoys doing it.

Video for Sheryl puts her personality in the forefront. Her clients use her because of her expertise and willingness to help when others are unwilling or afraid. She produces videos which give the answers that most real estate agents protect with their lives.

When looking at her business from the outside as a customer, she realized that real estate agents protect information that she as a customer would want to know.

Her goal is to produce valuable information that the customer needs to make an informed decision. By producing the information that others are scared to share, and revealing her personality at the same time, Sheryl shows clients what it is like to work with her.

This concept that Sheryl has pioneered, brings clients through agent referrals and through her network that match her working personality.

Sheryl's work with her clients, the content she produces, and her personality can be seen at http://www.Facebook.com/folsomhomes.

Additional Companies to Watch on Facebook

Throughout speaking and consulting we have been fortunate to work with business owners who desired to push their business to the next level.

We invite you to check out these companies on Facebook and see how they are using it to generate sales.

- http://www.facebook.com/BurlesonOrthodontics. Orthodontist using the power of Facebook to generate additional sales and referrals.
- http://www.facebook.com/gregorysphotographyinc. Facebook loves photos. Photographer Greg Loll uses the power of Facebook to generate sales and show off his portfolio.
- http://www.facebook.com/RenaissanceArtLeather. Hand made goods are always in fashion when they are unique. Check out the works of this hand crafted artist.
- http://www.facebook.com/StudySkillsforTeachers. Helping to educate the future of America. Check out this company and how they use Facebook to share and educate.
- http://www.facebook.com/SmilewithEd. Dentists can use the power of Facebook to increase the smile count.
- http://www.facebook.com/askhowie. Author & Speaker Howie Jacobson has regular discussions & helps his readers.

Addendum

Trying to cover all of the details of Facebook in one book is a huge task.

There were features of Facebook that we wanted to cover yet couldn't in the pages you have read.

In the following pages, we include additional materials on specific features that you can use to generate business.

How to Use a Little Used Feature of Facebook to Generate Interest in Your Product or Service

Events are a secret weapon that, once unlocked, will generate new exposure for your business. Many believe you have to have a special occasion to have an event or that it is only a "self-promoting" venue where you hard sale your prospects on using your product or service.

When used correctly, events provide opportunities for more sales as well as building a deeper relationship with your Fans and Friends who like your business. During the live events that we do, many ask the question:

"Why would you want to build a deeper relationship with your Fans?"

The answer is simple. The deeper your relationship with your Fans, the more sales you will make in the long run. Events can help you accomplish sales and relationship-building at the same time, regardless of what kind of business you have.

Let's take a look at the categories of events that Facebook has available, and discuss the models for success with events. Each event has a category and while not required aids when users are searching for events to join.

Event Type	Category
Select Category: Party Causes Education Meetings Music/Arts Sports Trips Other	Select Type: Study Group Class Lecture Office Hours Workshop

These categories provide ample opportunity for a business to provide value to their Fans.

Event Categories for Business

Setting up events doesn't have to be an ordeal. There are two main types of events that businesses can perform on Facebook.

Events can be categorized into two primary goals:

1. Online to Offline Events
2. Online to Online

Let's take a look at each of these event types and how you can use them to take your business to the next level.

Online to Offline Events

Using an event to drive traffic to your store is a great way to build a deeper relationship with your Fans.

One of our clients is a real estate agent who helps home owners with distressed properties avoid foreclosure.

While there are the traditional methods to reach home owners, these traditional methods often require contacting home owners one on one.

She decided to do an educational event on how to help home owners avoid foreclosure. We suggested that this client invite her prospects, friends, and even fellow real estate agents who have no desire to help distressed home owners.

As a result of this event, she was able to pick up multiple hot business leads that were ready to take action in one setting. Attendees of the event where able to share their comments directly on the Wall of the event, generating more results for her that she was able to follow-up with at a later date.

The event continues to live on as pictures of the event, videos, and discussions of what was talked about are shared on the event Wall.

This is just one example of how to use an online Facebook event to bring your friends and Fans to your physical location. Later, we will discuss additional strategies to get attendance to your event.

Online to Online Events

Facebook provides a wonderful opportunity to do events online. Your friends and Fans are already on the Internet, and keeping them in the comfort of their home and allowing them to find out more information about your company, product, or services will deepen your relationship with them.

These events can be on a variety of topics and can have clear calls to action to get your Fans or friends to take the next step in the relationship with your company.

We mention relationship frequently, because those on Facebook want to have a relationship on some level with your company and the products or services you offer.

My brother and I do online events on a near weekly basis. Our focus, as you may have guessed, has to deal with how to generate more business from Facebook.

Each call has a specific focus and goal. When doing online events, a few goals that you can accomplish can be the following:

- Generating sales for a new product or service
- Providing new information to current clients
- Getting your current clients to come to an offline event
- Motivating prospects and friends to refer additional clients who are interested in your product or service

One of the great aspects of online events is that if only one person shows up, it isn't embarrassing.

Facebook Fan Page Event Model

In many businesses, events can quickly become a cornerstone of sales and lead generation. Each event can have its own personality. There are literally dozens of different events a business can run.

The model for a successful Facebook event is below.

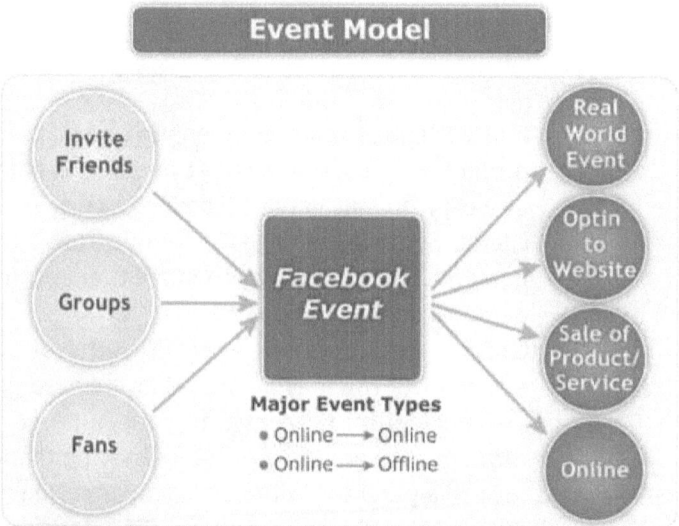

Every business should have a definition of success for each event.

One of the tasks that we recommend to our clients prior to putting events in place is to set goals for what they wish to have come out of each event.

The model can be used as a checklist for each event so that the maximum impact is gained from the effort that is put into it. Facebook has given events functionality that is on par with the Fan Page itself. In other words, you can post video, links, pictures, and have discussions centered on the event.

Finding Fans to Attend Your Event

The event model is driven from the point of getting Fans to the event from various traffic sources. The attendance sources that we reference in the model all exist within Facebook, however, you can and should involve prospects from as many sources as possible.

Let's take a look at the attendance sources outlined in the model above:

- **Invite friends** – many companies have personal profiles. Employees may have personal profiles, as well, who may very well be a source of clients. Sending messages to friends from personal profiles is a way to move them from personal contacts to business contacts.
- **Groups** – Groups can be a terrific source of attendance. You may be operating a Group right now and getting them over to your Fan Page through an event is a method to moving them toward a purchase with your company. One of our clients is a passionate corvette enthusiast. He has owned multiple corvettes during his life and his participation in these groups is a passion of his. His primary business is not corvettes; however, as a result of his participation in Groups, he gains attendance to his events through his participation.
- **Fans** – There is nothing like sending your Fans a message to let them know about an upcoming event. Many businesses travel to trade shows or festivals. Passionate customers crave information from your company. Letting them know where you are going to be and when the next opportunity to consume your information

is invaluable. With your Fans, you can geographically and demographically send them messages which can keep you from sending out repetitive information.

5 Rules for Having a Successful Event

As we discussed earlier, making each event a success is desirable because you are putting work into making the event happen.

After having conducted 100's of events ourselves, and having our clients conduct 1,000's of events, we have discovered some rules that we would invite you to consider putting into place for your own events.

1. **Make sure they have all of the information –** Your guests will want to know the information about the upcoming event. For example, we had a client once who forgot to put the physical address on the wall of the event. It was correctly listed in the event details; however, having the information in multiple places never hurt, as many of her guests were delayed.
2. **A picture is worth a thousand words –** People love pictures, and each event can have its own image associated with the event. By default, Facebook will give you an icon; however, it shows little effort if you don't take a few minutes to change the image out.
3. **Encourage guests to bring guests –** Nothing fills an event faster than having your guests bring an

additional guest. Many times people don't know they can bring one, so be upfront about who can attend.

4. **Keep it interesting** – Regardless of the event, with very few exceptions, keep the event focused on what people want. You want sales; however, people don't want to be sold something. Even a sales event at your physical store can be about the event itself, which will generate more sales for you.

5. **People forget, so remind them (nicely)** – The world of social media is no different than the real world where people forget the information. Reminding guests about your upcoming event is a nice way to make sure the event is a success. Be careful not to repeatedly remind your guests, as you will decrease their attention to your information.

There are times when an event doesn't go well. Sometimes there isn't the attendance you desire, and other times people just don't seem to respond well. Events are a great way to connect with your Fans, so don't get discouraged.

Let's get into even more details on events and putting them to work on behalf of your business.

Don't Leave Me Out!

No one likes to be left on the outside looking in, and with events, you can use this to your advantage. Events allow you to display the confirmed attendance to your event.

Knowing that certain important people are attending the "party" means others will want to be there. Sometimes, this just requires sending a simple direct message to those in your network you know have influence.

Below is a screen shot of what a confirmed guest list will look like. Drawing attention to guests through direct message, wall posts, and updates, signals to others that they don't want to be left out of the event.

Potential attendees to your event will see this upon landing on your event page, which we will cover in detail shortly. Having others help you increase the attendance to your event is even easier than just encouraging them to make wall posts.

When guests RSVP to your event, their action has the opportunity to show up in the News Feed of their friends. No one likes to be left out of the party, and Facebook knows this and provides a way for attendance to easily increase to your events.

In the screen below, Sam Spade (that is in fact his real name and not made up) put in his RSVP for an event that my brother and I were doing. What it also shows is the others in Sam's network who are attending the event.

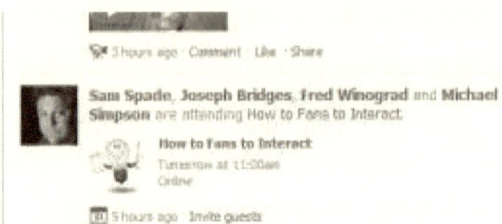

The notice to the Wall also provides an easy way to invite others to the event along with the title and image of the event.

Getting your Fans to RSVP for your events can create a viral following, so allowing enough time to market an event is key. This way it can routinely show up in your Fans' News Feeds as they RSVP for the event.

Advertising Your Event with Paid Ads

We get into a discussion on Facebook advertising in chapter X; however, it is worth a discussion here about advertising events. A quick look at an ad for event is below.

Facebook ads can advertise your event and provide potential Fans with two options. Viewers of the ad can choose to click the ad to see the full details of the ad, or they can RSVP directly from the ad.

In our testing, and that of our clients, we discovered that the cost for event advertising can vary across the board. When advertising for an event, we recommend watching the budget and RSVP's closely to get the maximum return on the money spent.

Getting the Most Out Of Your Event

Let's look at a screen shot of the event screen and additional features that can aid in the success of putting events into place in your business.

The screen shot below shows an event screen filled out with details that are important to the Fans who are interacting and taking part in the event. With events, the details add to the effectiveness of the system.

Event Details for Maximum Impact

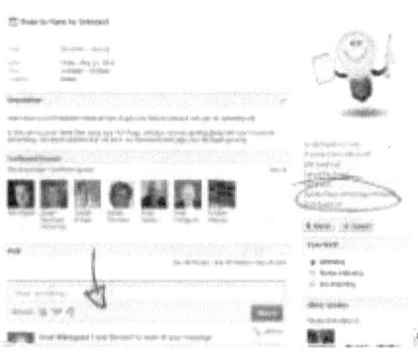

Event functions can be easily found in the right hand portion of the screen.

These are tools that you can use to get more Fans and friends to the event.

From the event, you can invite Fans of your page. When a user has a personal profile connected to their Fan Page, they also have the option to "invite people" which is their friend list via e-mail if they aren't connected to them in Facebook currently.

It is worth noting that inviting friends who are not already on Facebook via e-mail is a quick way to build your Fan list. While Facebook has hundreds of millions of users, there are still those out there who aren't on Facebook.

The Wall of an event screen (as noted by the down arrow in the screen shot above) is where Fans and the business can interact with each other. Attendees, and even those who can't make it, can post their comments of the event.

Encourage attendees, and even those that can't make it, to put up their comments, pictures, and videos. When you know of customers or prospects that enjoy participating in your events, reaching out to them in advance, or through a direct message, can be used to get the ball moving.

Updating Your Fans

Businesses that advertise nationally and have local events can target Fans via "Update Fans of…" functionality.

When looking at this feature, we would ask you to ask the question as follows:

"Do I like getting invited to events that I have no chance of being able to attend?"

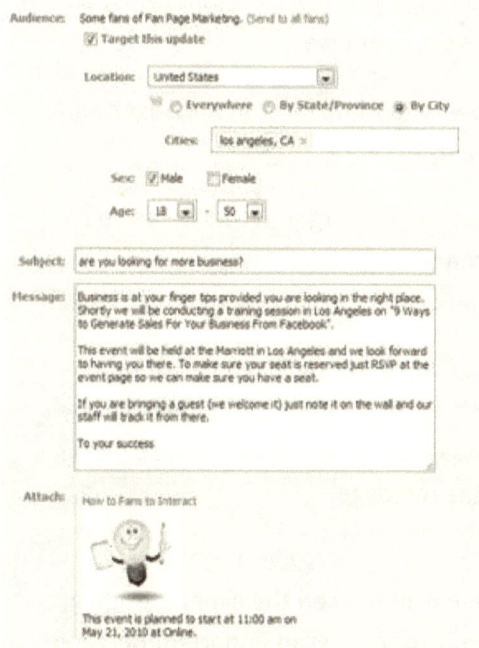

While being included is great, being invited to an event that you have no chance of making is no fun at all. My brother and I recently received an invitation to attend a live event in Texas with only 2 days notice. This didn't make us feel welcome. It made us feel like an afterthought. Making your Fans feel like an afterthought is not good for generating more business.

Businesses that conduct training events or have local events can use this functionality to their advantage.

My brother and I travel across the country training companies, businesses, and entrepreneurs on how to get the most out of their efforts on Facebook, so the ability to target our Fans is invaluable.

In the screen shot to the left, I took a sample message that we sent out to target just the Fans that would be most able to access the event we were doing.

Targeting Fans allows you to make your messages more personal and focused.

Businesses that have events targeted toward an age group or gender, can send direct messages to Fans that are in the target market they are trying to reach.

By targeting the messages, Fans will not get sent messages that don't appeal to them, and the response rate from your messages will be higher because of the targeted focus of the message.

What do your Fans do after the event?

After your Fans have experienced the event, deciding what action to take with them is an important decision. Those who are willing to attend events will be part of your most active Fan base. This means they are the most likely to do immediate business with your company, or refer customers to your company.

One of the great benefits of putting events into place to generate sales for your business, is you can print out the guest list of who attended the event and who said they were coming to the event.

There are many companies who prefer not to have attendees to their events "buy right now." The RSVP list provides an instant follow-up group for any sales staff or customer relations department.

One of our clients regularly hosts events, and uses the RSVP list to follow-up via direct message, comment, and call where the user has a phone number in the personal profile. For this particular client, 10% of his/her sales are generated from post event follow-up.

Event Disasters – How to Ruin an Event

Your Fans are waiting to come to your event, and they are going to have a great time interacting with you. There are some ways you can ruin an event that we would like to caution you against. Clients in the past have had events not go as well as planned with these methods.

- **Don't turn a training event into a pitch fest –** There are times when companies are doing an event to sell a product. There is nothing wrong with providing information and then offering attendees an opportunity to purchase a product from your company. When conducting an event online, or even in person, provide value to ALL those in attendance, not just the ones who purchase your product or service.
- **Failure to remind the attendees –** Many have assumed incorrectly that because someone RSVP's, they will put that in their calendar. Reminders via direct message, wall posts, status updates, and yes, the phone, can greatly

increase the attendance to the event.
- **Not making it easy to attend your event** – This applies to both online events and physical events. When conducting online events, if there is a conference line to call into, make the number clear by conference number, and time by time zone. For events at a physical location, providing directions with a screen shot of Google maps and easy directions to your facility will help make it easy for your guests.

Most of all, just be yourself at these events, and your business will generate while having fun with your clients.

Marketing Tab – Get People to "Like" Your Business

A Fan Page with people who "Like" it is much like a website without any visitors. It just doesn't work. Before you can start generating sales and leads, you have to have people who know about you on Facebook! While there are many methods (from paid advertising to guerilla marketing), the traffic won't convert unless you give people a powerful reason to click "Like". After all, once someone clicks "Like", they are in your world where you can share with them events, land in their News Feed, share status updates, and more.

With your website, you create landing pages where you can send focused traffic for specific keywords and terms, to convert traffic to sales and leads. With your

Fan Page, you create a marketing tab that converts traffic into friends for your business.

Currently, Facebook limits the number of businesses a user can "Like" to 500, which means that people won't click just any business. They need to see the value. Your marketing tab is your opportunity to share, in 10 seconds or less, why they should be part of your community.

Getting people into your business community may sound strange; however, Facebook embraces conversation among users. The more your Fan Page embraces the concept of conversation, the more success you will have. Your Fan Page will be exposed to all types of traffic, which is why your marketing landing tab will play such a pivotal role in getting people into the conversation. You can receive traffic from search engines, email marketing, your website, Twitter, and more. In order to capitalize on this traffic, we would invite you to consider making your marketing tab the default landing tab for anyone who does not currently "Like" your business.

Elements of a High Converting Marketing Tab

Styles of graphics, color schemes, and the like will vary differently depending on the type of business you operate. Some business owners look to continue their look and feel from their website, while others look to create a wildly different appearance for those who find them on Facebook. Regardless of the direction you decide to pursue, when you want to hit conversion rates of traffic that are upwards of 40%, we invite you to consider three key elements.

Call to Action

Your call to action is the most obvious item that you want a visitor to make. For many businesses, they will share their unique selling proposition here (USP), so visitors can immediately see the benefit in reading more about "why" they would take the time to click "Like". Your call to action should share with a new visitor in less than 10 seconds why they would want to join in your conversation. No need for a giveaway (although that can work). Simply reveal the benefits of connecting with your business.

Visual Cues – Get Your Graphic Guy Working Away

Facebook allows you to load your landing page with video, graphics, copy and more. Take full advantage of this by having your graphics point out the obvious fact that you want people to click "Like". Attention spans of people online (and even offline, for that matter) are short, so don't waste any real estate by having them guess where to click. For many people, the concept of clicking "Like" is so new they get lost on what to do. Make it easy on them!

Once They Click "Like", Capitalize On Their Attention

A high converting landing tab is only part of your first moments when a visitor sees your Fan Page. As your landing tab converts visitors into new friends, you now have more of their attention. Attention is valuable when used correctly.

The model below will demonstrate the goal path of your first experience with your Facebook user.

The options that you have once you begin the relationship are limitless.

How Can A Stupid Mobile Phone Generate More Sales When the Customer Is Standing In Front Of You?

By James and Joey Bridges

When you have a physical location, it can cost good money to get people to come through the doors. Whether you operate a hair salon, hobby store, chiropractic office, or any other business, having people come to you is both a revenue opportunity and an expense.

With your marketing in place, you could have 100, 200, and even over 400 people weekly come through your doors. Wouldn't it be nice if you could maximize the dollar value of each person? Why settle for an average sale when you can add a little more value and make 50% more money?

There isn't a need to put them under a heat lamp to make more money. No high pressure sales tactics needed. You don't even need to attend a seminar to discover new "objection handling" methods. You can actually get customers to help you sell more by empowering them to use an item that nearly everyone carries with them...their mobile phone.

With five billion mobile phones worldwide today, there are good odds that your customer has one. People are on their phones constantly. Most of the time they are on their phone when you don't want them to be! You might be telling them about their next appointment, and they are barely paying attention because they are texting a friend. You might even be attempting to give them a discount on their purchase, and yet they are too pre-occupied with what is happening on Facebook to even notice. If only there was a way to tap into that usage quickly and easily. More on that later.

Missed Customer Opportunity

The most valuable customer is the one you already have. With the customer acquisition rates rising, some studies say it has tripled over the last 10 years. Getting your current customers to invest more is essential.

Many customers would invest more if asked. Many customers would actually bring you more business if it was easier to refer people to you. For business owners, the problem of getting more business out of their client base usually comes down to two major challenges.

1. Cost of new marketing
2. Time to put new marketing into action

Getting more business is great. Getting more business with expensive marketing is a waste. When you can tap into nearly free marketing, you will get more out of those great customers because you have a winning formula.

Your business is likely already busy with customers. You have them coming in regularly, and having the time to put a new system in may seem impossible. Sure, you notice your receptionist has some downtime, but can she put a new marketing system into action? Will it only last for a few days because she hopes you will forget about it?

Instead of wasting thousands of dollars with a new, over the top, expensive customer retention program, why not consider something different? Why not consider a solution that will make your receptionist (or front desk person) thrilled that you came up with something fun that makes you money?

Facebook Places – Cheap Mobile Marketing To Generate More Sales

With over 600+ million people on Facebook, you have a great opportunity since your customers not only have a cell phone, but you know where they check-in daily. Facebook has over 150 million people using their application on their mobile phones, and that number grows by the day (both internationally and domestic).

How do you tap into this massive user base when a customer is standing at your place of business?

Facebook Places is a powerful and free application that Facebook users can use to "check-in" to share that they are at your place of business. They can share with the world their activity. You might be thinking, who cares?

Picture this; someone comes to your Veterinarian office. They have a sick kitten (Who doesn't want to help a kitten?). You quickly discover that someone misdiagnosed the kitten, you prescribe new medicine and send the happy owner and pet on their way. What is the value of that story being shared? Better, what if that person sent a picture of the happy pet with everyone they knew on Facebook and they gave you the credit for the help?

How much would you pay for someone to send out a great story like that to 100 of their closest pet-loving friends? Would you pay $100? $250? More?

What if you didn't have to pay anything? What if you just asked your customer to share that story from their phone?

Facebook Places is one of the newest features of Facebook. It taps into the power of mobile phones and allows people to share where they are, what they are doing, and more. Most business owners simply "hope" that people will talk about their business. Instead of hoping people will share great stories, upload pictures, and provide feedback, why not make it easier on them?

Although there are over a dozen different ways to get the most out of Facebook Places, we invite you to consider the following methods to jump starting your business success.

- **Ask Your Customers to Share** – People will share when you give them an opportunity. When a customer is in front of you, ask them to share their experience. You can even have a list of common great items they can share with their "friends". By having a list of great items to share, customers can't escape with "writers block" excuses.

- **Engage Your Customers** – Facebook is about conversation. Just letting your customers "check-in" is only a one way conversation. Go to your Facebook Places page and comment on the customers who came by. Share a note, an observation, or even a link to your website where they can find even more values.
- **Take Ownership of Your Page** – As a business owner, you can take ownership of your page. It gives you additional permissions and control. Many businesses currently have Places that they no one owns. It's free to take ownership; you just have to find your place of business on Facebook.

Facebook Places will give you the edge in mobile marketing. It's easy to put into action, and makes it fun to get more business. Your staff likes to be on Facebook. Your customers like to be on Facebook. Give your staff and customers the power to bring you more business today by putting Facebook Places marketing into action.

How To Use Facebook Deals To Generate More Business Now

By Jamey and Joey Bridges

Envision yourself walking through a store. The store that you are walking through is one you might commonly browse. You really want to see the new products available. The store could be a local sporting goods store, hobby store, or even a boutique retailer.

As you are walking around checking out the different items, you take out your phone to see what is happening on Facebook. The News Feed shares a variety of interesting stories. You want to see who else is nearby just in case they have time for a quick chat or coffee. To see the latest locations of your friends, you review the Places feature on your Facebook application.

Facebook Places provides you with your friend's information and something more. It is showing you additional stores that are nearby, encouraging you to "check-in".

The best part is that Facebook Places is providing you a deal. Yes, a simple free application could give you 50% off or even donate to your favorite charity.

How?

Facebook Places, although initially developed to allow users to share their location, has grown. A business owner can target users on their mobile phones, get them to interact with their business, and offer them "deals".

Everyone loves a deal. Everyone loves saving money on a purchase. It doesn't have to be big savings; just the art of saving money or getting a better value on an item can push any of us into taking action. Facebook Places allows you the option of providing a deal to any prospect that "checks-in" to your business.

Facebook Places In A Nutshell

Facebook Places provides you the power of targeting users who use their mobile phones. There are over 200 million users currently using the Facebook mobile application. It is one of the largest segments of users.

According to Facebook, mobile users are twice as active as ones who just use a computer.

Tapping into a user base that is two times as active increases the chance of a sale for a business owner. A local business can combine their places page and their Fan Page for additional functionality. These businesses end up with an extremely powerful marketing platform.

Imagine that a potential customer that searches on their computer or on their mobile phone can find the best deals available at your store!

Facebook Deals

Currently, Facebook Deals aren't available to every business. In the initial roll-out, the opportunity to offer prospective customers "deals" was only available to big companies. Companies like Chipotle, the North Face, 24 Hour Fitness and others jumped on the opportunity to offer "deals". Deals ranged from a $1 donation to two entrees for the price of one.

Although initially only available to a set of preferred partners, Facebook Deals, is now available to the rest of us. Because you will be able to target users based on their location relative to your store, Facebook wants to ensure you are a "real business." Quite simply, this means that you must prove:

1. You have a real physical location
2. You are the business owner

Although these requirements sound simple, they ensure that fake stores won't confuse customers. Facebook is going to lengths of validating business licenses and even electrical bills to ensure that only valid businesses get the opportunity to offer deals.

Once you get accepted to offer Deals, your opportunity of marketing will fall into four types of deals.

Individual Deals

When you want to offer something special as a one-time offering to new customers, existing customers, or just to encourage more people to visit your store, then this will be the type of deal to offer. Individual deals are a great way to engage new prospects. Get them used to the concept that "deals" will be available when they use their phone at your location.

Loyalty Deals

Do you have those customers that you are happy to see each time they walk into your store? Those customers who spend consistently and are happy to refer you are a great sight! Reward those customers who invest in your business frequently. With Loyalty Deals, you have the opportunity to offer something special. A business owner can change the offer to those who have checked-in more than twice and no more than 20 times.

Friend Deals

One customer is nice, but eight at the same time are better. What would you offer that customer who brings in seven of their closest friends? Would you offer them a free drink? Maybe you would offer a round of drinks for the entire group? With Friend Deals, you can offer something special for groups up to eight people.

Charity Deals

Would you like to let customers know that you aren't just about profits? Want to support a charity that you have a passion for? With Charity Deals, you get the opportunity to support the charity of your choice for each person that will "check-in" at your location.

Four deal options provide each business owner with flexibility. The flexibility and the simplicity of the offerings allow you to engage prospects. Engaging prospects & customers compels them to action.

As you consider what deal you might offer with your business, reflect on the following guidelines:

1. What do your customers crave?
2. What will make your customers share this deal with their friends?
3. What deal will make customers eager to speak with you when they are in your store?

An added benefit of "deals" is that it generates conversation. The most successful deals will generate conversation both online and offline. A deal can be created in **7 simple steps**, which gives you the opportunity to change deals as your store and the market change. Keep your prospective customers eager to come back by putting in a simple plan of changing your deals!

Get the shortcut to beating your competition by putting Deals into action for your business. By starting a Fan Page, a Places Page, and applying for Deals, you will be able to start generating more sales today with Facebook's marketing methods. The best part is they are all free to start; you just have to put them into action.

About Todd Bates

As a pioneer in the marketing field, Todd has created 47 different companies that have helped small businesses put strategies into action that quickly increase their sales. He is well known for his ability to get attendees to overcome their fears to take their business to the next level. Specializing in direct response marketing, sales conversion methods, and social marketing strategies, Todd has a passion for helping individuals and businesses improve their bottom line.

Todd's direct and "over the top" style in speaking brings audiences to life and prepares them to take action. Attendees laugh as they discover his methods and feel like they are the only one in the room. By the end, they have clear action items that they can take home to improve their sales.

Since 1990 Todd has been sharing his strategies with individuals and small business owners. He has shared his methods and techniques with over 250,000 people through his speaking events. A dedication to helping people in his unique one on one style has allowed him to help over 20,000 individual business owners.

About James & Joey Bridges

With a background in IT that started from their days at the University of Southern California, James and Joey have been developing Internet based solutions for over 14 years.

As consultants to major Fortune 500 companies, they developed web based systems that increased productivity and profitability.

During their time as consultants, they taught as instructors in the Internet Technology Program at the University of Southern California for six years.

Starting in 2003, they created a real estate company that sold over 100 million dollars in real estate from the Internet. This company continues to operate today without the daily management of James and Joey.

Since 2007, James and Joey have launched additional online businesses, and in 2009 built a seven figure coaching and training business in seven months.

Assisting small business owners generate sales from Facebook has been their passion since late 2007. They have developed models for business owners to grow their sales through the of Facebook, and they share these while speaking and training across the United States. Find the latest adventures of James and Joey on Facebook at www.Facebook.com/FanPageSystem.

.

Special Gifts from the Authors

A Special FREE Gift from the Authors

To Help You Get The Most Out Of This Book There is a Collection of

FREE Extra Resources Waiting For you at:

www.ToddBatesBook.com/Resources

- Complete audio training course done by the author to help you overcome your E.I.D.
- Checklists to help you conquer Facebook and build your business the right way
- How to find your niche and dominate it in 90 days on Facebook
- Exclusive access to the authors with a special coaching coupon to get your questions answered

1 on 1 Business Planning Session with Business & Marketing Coach Todd Bates

Change the course of your business forever with a private one on one session with 7 figure net income entrepreneur Todd Bates

www.ToddBatesSystems.com

- A private session with Todd Bates to discuss any business issue you have in your business.
- Find out how you can generate more leads that you can turn into sales in your business.
- Discover opportunities that you are missing in your business right now.
- Get connected to Todd's inner circle of students and mastermind members who can help grow your business.

"Join Our Podcast For That Provides Weekly Help For the Busy E.I.D Entrepreneur With our Weekly High Energy, Power Packed, & Informative Systems"

Weekly We Deliver Information To Help Entreprenuers Increase Their Business on The Internet

Subscribe for FREE to the Podcast today by visiting:

www.FBSmallBusiness.com

- Each session provides specific action items for you to put into place in your business.
- Lessons designed to get you generating sales not wasting time.
- High energy and designed for businesses of all levels

www.ingramcontent.com/pod-product-compliance
Lightning Source LLC
Chambersburg PA
CBHW030942180526
45163CB00002B/676